W9-DGL-787

INTERNATIONAL
EXCELLENCE

Also by Christopher Engholm
Doing Business in the New Vietnam (1995)
The Asia and Japan Business Information Sourcebook (1994)
Doing Business in Asia's Booming "China Triangle" (1994)
*The Other Europe: A Complete Guide to Business Opportunities
in Eastern Europe* (1993)
*When Business East Meets Business West: The Guide to
Practice and Protocol in the Pacific Rim* (1992)
*The China Venture: America's Corporate Encounter with
the People's Republic of China* (1991)

Also by Diana Rowland
*Japanese Business Etiquette: A Practical Guide to Success
with the Japanese* (1993)

INTERNATIONAL EXCELLENCE

*Seven Breakthrough Strategies
for Personal and Professional Success*

Christopher Engholm
and Diana Rowland

KODANSHA INTERNATIONAL
NEW YORK • TOKYO • LONDON

HD
62.4
E54
1996

Kodansha America, Inc.
114 Fifth Avenue, New York, New York 10011, U.S.A.

Kodansha International Ltd.
17–14 Otowa 1-chome, Bunkyo-ku, Tokyo 112, Japan

Published in 1996 by Kodansha America, Inc.

Library of Congress Cataloging-in-Publication Data

Engholm, Christopher.
International excellence: seven breakthrough strategies for
personal and professional success / Christopher Engholm and
Diana Rowland.
p.   cm.
Includes bibliographical references.
ISBN 1-56836-082-7
1. International business enterprises—Management.
2. Intercultural communication.   3. Success in business.
I. Rowland, Diana.   II. Title.
HD62.4.E54   1994
658'.049—dc20   95-36818

Book design by Charles Davey *design lab*

Printed in the United States of America

96 97 98 99 00 BER/B 10 9 8 7 6 5   4 3 2 1

CONTENTS

INTERNATIONAL
EXCELLENCE

INTRODUCTION

"Globalization" has become the sexiest new business trend—at least in the public relations departments of Fortune 500 firms. IBM now provides "solutions for a small planet." Ford has "used global thinking to create a car just right for the world today." Xerox is now "The (I need it printed in Hong Kong by two o'clock their time, which is right now our time) company." And Bill Marriott boasts that "since today's business buzz word is 'global,' it's a good thing we already are."

Unfortunately, many of us are not. Many of us have been caught off guard by the sudden internationalization of jobs, technology, and money. Many of us are unprepared to think about our careers and our businesses in nondomestic terms. Few of us have long experience working with people from other cultures, or working *for* them. The rules we follow suddenly don't apply when we engage in business outside our borders. Business practices and behaviors alienate us, and ours seem to irritate our counterparts. They negotiate differently. The protocol is abstruse. We throw up our arms and say it's not worth the effort.

But . . . other firms seem to be making a lot of money "out there." And so-and-so just got hired by that hot new software firm because "he knew how to deal with the Malaysians." Like it or not, it's time to build up your international skills—to become internationally excellent.

Slouching Towards Globalism

As recently as 1985, as American businesses merged and acquired each other in a shameful denial of mounting international competition, the most widely read book about revitalizing corporate America—*Reinventing the Corporation,* by John Naisbitt and Patricia Aburdene—didn't even mention the need for American corporations to internationalize. Meanwhile, Japan's powerful *sōgō shōsha* (general trading companies) were being reshaped into *kokusai sōgō kigyō,* globally integrated corporations. Japan's Canon was suddenly selling 80 percent of its output overseas; Matsushita was employing one-third non-Japanese workers; and because of the high yen, Honda was manufacturing overseas and reexporting cars back to the Japan market.

New players from Britain, Taiwan, Korea, Thailand, Iran, Saudi Arabia, Japan, and the Netherlands set up plants in inexpensive America, and shipped billions of dollars in profits back home. In 1980, foreigners owned only 2 percent of the U.S. economy; a decade later, they owned 14 percent. To our collective dismay, America's two most potent rivals in the coming global shakeout were already claiming victory. In the Japanese version of the controversial book *The Japan That Can Say No,* the authors predicted that military might wouldn't mean much in the economic war of the twenty-first century, and that Japan would be victorious in that war. West German Chancellor Helmut Kohl predicted recently that "the 1990s will be the decade of the Europeans and not that of the Japanese." (He didn't even mention the Americans.) And Italy's foreign minister and rotating head of the European Economic Community (EEC), Gianni De Michelis, proclaimed that Japan's shortcomings will come to the surface in the next 10 years, and that Europe will recover "its role as the core of the world economy." To the spokespeople of our global competitors, American renewal and influence isn't even considered a possibility.

Finally, a reluctant America has begun to shift from being a self-sufficient national economy to an interdependent one existing in a globally integrated economy. American managers and entrepreneurs are at last realizing that they need to respond to rising global competition, and need to do so urgently. Americans suddenly understand that a superpower is only as mighty as the ability of its corporations to operate (and cooperate) internationally. And that corporations are only as strong as the ability of their workforces to cross national and cultural boundaries and function in the global marketplace.

Coca-Globalization. Corporate sales figures show that the global thrust is real. In 1980, Proctor & Gamble sold 32 percent of its total production output overseas; now its foreign sales make up 53 percent of the total. With the end of the Cold War, Hughes Space & Communications Company set out to reproportion its lopsided ratio of government contract work versus foreign-customer commercial work, and the company has surpassed its goal during the past five years. Ford Motor Company's business with Japanese companies, said to be greater than any other firm's, was causing it to purchase 8,000 or so U.S.-Japan round-trip airline tickets each year, says a consultant for the company. And Coca-Cola was suddenly selling *two-thirds* of its beverages outside the United States.

By 1986, Coke had racked up cash reserves of $1.5 billion, but instead of spending the money to acquire subsidiaries or repurchasing company stock, as other Fortune 500 companies were doing, Coke's globally wise president, vice president, and chief financial officer—Goizueta, Keogh, and Ivester, respectively—set about achieving the company's ultimate mission of "worldwide soft drink saturation." This would be achieved through a strategy encapsulated in a slogan coined by Goizueta: "Availability, Affordability, and Acceptability." The mission was to make Coke affordable to everyone, to every person on earth, whether they were above or below the poverty line. Implementation of the strategy would vary in each country, "depending on the culture, economy, and stage of industrial development." For example, in China and Indonesia the company would set up the infrastructure for selling Coca-Cola, including the building of concentrate factories, glass manufacturers, bottling plants, trucks, point-of-purchase signs, and the like. On the other hand, in Germany the challenge would be to consolidate 96 different established bottlers, many of whom were competing against one another in small territories. Long before it became a bumper sticker, Keogh and Goizueta coined a slogan for their strategy: "Think globally, but act locally."[1]

The New Globalists. As we move from mass production to customization, from mass marketing to microniche marketing, from the corporate monolith to networks of enterprises, we shift away from smokestack industries such as steel, oil, and heavy manufacturing to "soft" industries such as media, computers, software, and communications. With this shift, smaller companies have entered the global fray. An unassuming microenterprise can now be a global competitor.

And they can come from anywhere. In 1970, the United Nations Center on Transnational Corporations tallied 7,000 multinational corporations (MNCs) around the world, with over half headquartered in the United States and Britain. Now, in the mid-1990s, there are 35,000 MNCs, with the United States, Japan, Germany, and Switzerland accounting for fewer than half of them.

What's Driving Internationalization?

Contrary to what isolationists in Washington would have you think, seeking out cheap exploitable labor in Third World banana republics is a fading factor in the new age of corporate globalization. In fact, there isn't space in this book to cover all the reasons a firm goes global in the 1990s, but there are a few you should be aware of. One is that globalization reduces a company's exposure to political instability, changing markets, currency fluctuations, and other unknowns. In the 1980s, for instance, IBM divided itself into two halves: Domestic (the United States) and World Trade (everywhere else). "This provides an insurance," says IBM international sales veteran David Mercer, "that IBM is never exposed to insurmountable problems with a single source of supply on any product; there is always the fall-back of the sister plant(s) in the other half of the corporation."

Second, the world's largest multinational firms headquartered in the West have witnessed local competitors in Asia and Latin America becoming formidable threats. Fast-growing foreign companies you probably haven't heard about—because they aren't yet listed on any stock exchange—already possess webs of closely held assets and a roster of local, regional, and Western joint venture partners. Some have the capital to finance their own future expansion, a large number of them are supported by their governments, and all are intent on keeping outside firms from Europe, Japan, and America from stealing their local markets. What happens when one of those companies suddenly floods your markets with low-priced, high-quality goods?

One strategy is to acquire control of the company through stock ownership and/or equity joint ventures. This strategy became popular in the 1980s among U.S. automakers losing ground to Japanese and Korean automakers. General Motors' joint venture with Toyota was formed, in part, so that GM could control—or co-opt—Toyota's share of the U.S. market. In Poland, for example, Pepsi-Cola purchased 40 percent of the widely known confectionery factory Wedel, now listed on the Warsaw Stock Exchange. In Czechoslovakia, Proctor & Gamble entered an accord to acquire Rakona, a detergents enterprise, for $20 million.

The need for capital is a third driving force. A risky venture may not find venture capital in the risk-averse West; a wealthy Indonesian business family or Korean *cheabol*, or corporate conglomerate, might be a better bet. Disney found this out when Prince Al-Walid bin Talal bin Abdul-Aziz Al-Saud, who lives in a 130-room palace in Riyadh, injected $400 million to bail out Euro Disney, now called Disneyland Paris—acquiring 24 percent of the venture. As one would expect, the new billionaires hail from the newly emerging economies of Latin America and the Far East. They include people like Korean Shin Kyuk-ho (worth $6 billion) and Emilio Azcarraga Milmo of Mexico (worth $5.1 billion). In Mexico, beer baron Pablo Aramburuzabala cut a deal with Anheuser-Busch, Carlos Gonzalez struck a retailing deal with Price Club, and baker Lorenzo Servitgie inked a distribution deal with Sara Lee.

Fourth, rising standards of world-class manufacturing are forcing manufacturers to think globally. As technological innovation becomes more globalized, many firms have entered overseas regions like Japan, Taiwan, and Europe simply for technological survival; those that don't may find their products will soon become obsolete. Few believed China capable of producing products indistinguishable from those made in Singapore or elsewhere; now the country's trade surplus has ballooned because of it. Technology-hungry Japanese firms have been taking advantage of the power of America's melting-pot research-and-development sector for decades, and American firms are learning to do the same.

Emerging Market Fever. Since the fall of the Berlin Wall and the dismantling of the Soviet Union, the world economy has undergone a dramatic change. Business executives, entrepreneurs, and stock investors now talk about high-growth "emerging markets" as often as they talk about the traditional economies of the developed world. And well they should. By the year 2010, three-fourths of world trade growth will come from so-called emerging countries like Poland, China, Brazil, and Russia. China now purchases over $10 billion worth of American products per year, including 14 percent of Boeing's aircraft sales, which support the jobs of 200,000 Americans at home. In 1993, developing countries attracted a combined total of $130 billion in foreign investment. The emerging nations of East-Central Europe alone are home to 105 million people, who have been shut out of Western markets for decades and who literally *need everything.*

American marketers often ask senator-turned-business-consultant Gary Hart whether their companies' goods and services are needed in East Europe. Again and again, he tells them: "The East Europeans need everything, not only in goods, but also in services. They need pollution-control equipment, they need technology, they need training, food, fuel, medicine. You name it, they need it. It's a wide-open, brand-new market, and the same can be said in spades for the former Soviet Union."

As part of the Clinton administration's National Export Strategy, the U.S. Department of Commerce recently issued a report about the so-called big emerging markets, or BEMs. The report stated that while the large industrialized nations of the world economy "will continue to be the largest U.S. markets for decades to come," the emerging economies of the world hold "far more promise for large incremental gains in U.S. exports." BEMs already purchase about one-quarter of America's exports, well over $100 billion worth each year, and account for over 40 percent of world imports (excluding the United States). Moreover, emerging stock markets have captivated enormous numbers of both institutional and individual investors in the United States.

Emerging countries drive globalization of business activities because they tend to demand that foreign companies set up a representative office—if not a factory—as part of a quid pro quo for gaining market access. These countries have studied success stories such as those of Malaysia, Taiwan, Singapore, and China, all of which allowed foreign investors to profit in their economies but asked in return that they share ownership of ventures, transfer technology, train workers and managers—that is, become local corporate citizens. Direct exports to these countries is no longer a viable way to capture market share in these high-growth areas. It takes total engagement to succeed.

What This Book Will Do for You

International Excellence is for anyone whose job (or job aspirations) requires that he or she effectively communicate, negotiate, and socialize with people in the global marketplace. We hope to inspire readers to "go global"—in both their professional and personal lives —by providing seven core strategies for crossing cultural barriers and achieving financial success anywhere in the world.

Based on our international corporate seminar programs, the book offers practical guidance to help American businesspeople cross borders adroitly, and thus gain an edge over their competitors. This book provides you with the tools to respond creatively to the challenges faced in the international marketplace today, to sharpen your communicating and negotiating skills, to deal with differing ethical systems, and to acquire "protocol power" wherever you are.

The state of being "internationally excellent" requires that a person possess three things: (1) *awareness* of cultural and business differences among overseas counterparts; (2) *skills* for working with these differences; and (3) *experience* in international settings. The first has to do with gaining knowledge about a foreign culture, about how it functions, how its businesspeople negotiate, and how they deal with Westerners; the second refers to the techniques one needs to bridge cultures, communicate with the locals, understand their nonverbal signals, counter their deal-making strategies, and conduct oneself according to the fine points of overseas etiquette and protocol; and the third involves putting the first two elements to work in the field.

Any person can learn the necessary skills to personally excel in an integrated world. You don't have to be cosmopolitan or super-sophisticated, nor do you have to live overseas for years or work for an internationalized company; but you *do* have to be savvy.

In this regard, the authors would like to thank the numerous people, both here and abroad, who have shared with us their experiences and insights into international business practices and customs. We are particularly indebted to Richard J. Barnet, Franck Burham, Barbara Chronowski, Donald P. Brown, Fred Burke, David F. Day, Harvey Goldman, Doris Gottlieb, John L. Graham, Scott Grimes, John A. Haglund, Roger A. Harris, Li Wo Hing, Ken Jacobson, Harbo Jensen, Colleen Kelley, John Konrad, Thomas Lifson, Mike Lorelli, Antoine Morrison, Kamal Naffa, Bill Pomeranz, Karen Rakita, Ronn Richard, Tamera Richardson, Marlene Rossman, John So, Paul Solman, and Stewart D. Stemple.

We would also like to express thanks to the other people who made this book possible, including our agent, Julie Castiglia; Philip Turner and Joshua Sitzer, our editors at Kodansha America; Harvey Goldman for his expert insights and editorial advice; Marlene Rossman for her professional and personal contributions; Jeanie Engholm for typing the manuscript; and David Fletcher, for his tireless editorial effort on this project.

Adopting a Global Vision

Mike Lorelli had won his promotion working for the Pepsi Corporation's Pizza Hut division. He was now president of international operations at a company doing business in 78 countries around the world. Soon after Lorelli had his new office arranged, he received word that he'd be leaving on an overseas business trip to solidify relationships with Pizza Hut affiliates. He was gone for the better part of nine months, during which time he "clocked forty countries in regions all around the world."

"In some cases we hit 13 countries in a 14-day period," he says. "We really beat our bodies up, but you've got to do it to start the relationships and truly understand what's going on."

Many extension pages to his *three* passports later, Lorelli returned a seasoned globalist, having come to realize that acquiring international savvy requires serious attention. "It wasn't just a matter of learning about geography," he says, "but in advance, truly understanding the cultures, the people, and how I would have to adapt my behavior for different situations so I would be perceived correctly, as opposed to being perceived as an Ugly American."

Claiming Your Stake in the Global Age

How many of us will find ourselves in Mike Lorelli's shoes at some time in our careers? If labor statistics are any clue, many of us will be making a career move into the global job market in the future. Expatriate hiring is on the rise even as U.S. firms have downsized. Of 120 U.S. companies recently surveyed, 61 percent say they employ more expats than they did five years ago. There are now

300,000 foreign workers in Japan, many of them Americans. The opening of the vast China market has increased the number of Americans living in Hong Kong to nearly 30,000, almost double the number a decade ago and higher than the number of British living in their former colony. In 1989 there were only 100 Americans living in the Czech Republic; now there are over 30,000. The Census Bureau estimates that as many as 250,000 U.S. citizens move out of the United States to live abroad each year; this figure was only 160,000 a year in 1980. (Ten percent of U.S. expatriates are female, up 5 percent in the past few years.)

International-related jobs are not only proliferating, they pay more too. According to the Labor Department, export-related jobs pay, on average, 20 percent higher wages than those jobs related only to the domestic economy. We are also more likely to be working for foreign-owned companies in this country. Foreign companies employ 4.9 million Americans in the United States; two million of these are high-wage manufacturing jobs in foreign affiliates set up on U.S. soil. That's roughly *one in ten* manufacturing jobs in the United States.

Domestic career strategies that may have worked well in the past may now be a formula for failure. Globalization means not only operating and marketing in unfamiliar cultural settings; it also means that here at home our organizations are becoming more culturally diverse. Like Mike Lorelli, we need to quickly acquire new skills to be successful in the new global environment.

In the past, executives with true global vision were born, not trained. Konosuke Matsushita was born with global vision; when he wrote his firm's business plan, it forecast company activities for the next 250 years!

Some readers might identify more closely with Mike Lorelli, who *fell* into a global position, and had to rise to the occasion. Lorelli had to acquire a global perspective because he was given a global position and he needed vision to make it work.

Western and Eastern *Weltanschauungs*

To broaden our individual mindsets, we need to get in touch with the most basic and submerged aspects of our worldview. Every culture embodies a unique conception of the world. As Americans, our *weltanschauung* rests on a desire to control, subdue, or dominate nature—to change it to accommodate man. In the garden of Eden, you might remember, God said to Adam and Eve: "Multiply and fill the earth and *subdue* it." Conversely, Eastern man (the Chinese, Japanese, Koreans) learned to accept nature, to work with it and adjust to it, in order to carry out the agricultural activities that allowed for survival. The early divinational religions of the East, including Taoism, were based on the concept of endless cyclical "change," as represented in the natural world and upon which their rice cultivation depended. Their universal conception was that man was to *adapt* to the constant change of nature and that trying to stop the change was as foolish as believing Yin would not progress inevitably to its opposite Yang.

Similar to the Eastern idea of adaptation to change, at least in this sense, was the Islamic notion of one's destiny being predetermined by fate. Man could only wait for the force of Allah to decide what his next move would be. Omar Khayyam, the twelfth-century Persian astronomer-poet, wrote in the *Rubaiyat:* "Yea, the first Morning of Creation wrote / What the Last Dawn of Reckoning shall read." Not much about becoming "a master of all the fish and birds and animals" in that line!

Let's take this a step further.

Americans learn from infancy that hard work equals success; children's books such as *The Little Engine That Could* inculcate this value. We laud striving, *self*-determination rather then determination by supernatural forces. You wouldn't expect an Arab to be striving and achievement-motivated, since he perceives fate to be beyond human control; change itself is tightly controlled and guided in the Middle East by ideological vision. So, too, personal striving is not common in North Africa, where tribal beliefs tend to put one's fate beyond one's control. What effects might our "man over nature" ethos have on our ability to globalize our perspectives? For starters, such an outlook makes it difficult for us to respond and adapt to global realities without wanting to change (subdue) them. For example, American executives tend to try to change rules in a foreign locale rather than accept them and play by them like everyone else. In sharp contrast, the "harmonizing" Japanese try to adapt and mold their approach and practices to fit with the requisites of the local scene. Our typical response to overseas problems is to ask for the rules of the playing field to be rewritten, or to send in the Marines.

Another ramification of this difference is mindset: the Easterner tends to seek agreements based on compromise, while the Westerner seeks to win by persuasion. Ancient traditional Indonesian village law (*adat*), for example, also put a premium on the concept of mutual assistance (*gotong royong*)—collaborative village effort, concern for the community, teamwork, and mutually beneficial win/win relationships.

America the Parochial

True globalism was never part of our country's heritage. America thought of itself as exceptional, a land of the future, of new ideas, far and away more culturally relevant than any other country could be. Our expansionism was carried forward in evangelical rather than territorial terms. We did not endeavor to "carve up" China or Cuba or the Philippines. When we declared war against the Spanish in 1898, it was to help them be more like us. Woodrow Wilson pledged to make the world safe for democracy, our system of governing. In 1940, Senator Kenneth Wherry of Nebraska epitomized our self-obsessed cultural imperialism when he said, "With God's help, we will lift Shanghai up and up, ever up, until it is just like Kansas City."

After World War II, we became more global in perspective, but this perspective was limited to a bicameral notion of East versus West. Michael Elliott has written in *Newsweek* in January 1995 that "the Cold War was oddly comfortable. We knew our place; knew who are friends and enemies were. . . . The global economic boom is uncomfortable, just as it was before World War I when technology and trade integrated the world economy as never before. Then it was Europe that felt the chill, as cheap American goods filled the stores. Now many in the United States see 'globalization' as a threat. India used to be a place whose teaming millions sometimes starved. Now it's a country whose textiles industries (and, within a decade, software houses) sell their low-cost goods to American markets."

Richard Barnet and John Cavanagh have recently written that "the leading industrial nations that formed a global alliance to oppose [the Soviet Union] have turned inward."[1] Americans, we would argue, suffer from cultural inwardness now more than ever. Hundreds of millions of people in the world speak at least some form of English, but of the 4,000 to 5,000 languages spoken on earth, the vast majority of Americans can speak only one of them. How unrealistic it is to watch a Federal Express 1994 television advertisement that features a Japanese executive crooning into the phone, "Harowwww," to an impatient American, as if large numbers of Japanese executives didn't speak English. In reality, very few American businesspeople speak enough Japanese to even say hello in Japanese. Only 71,000 Americans are currently studying abroad, and over 70 percent of them are in Europe; Asians, on the other hand, make up 59 percent of the 439,000 foreign students studying in the United States.

Adopting a Universal Perspective

Free trade deals like NAFTA, the European Union, and GATT won't erase borders or national priorities, or synthesize the world's economic systems into one World Economic System. The World Trade Organization, created by GATT to manage the opening of markets everywhere, suffered a stormy—and quite telling—beginning, with the Americans, Europeans, and Asians all pushing different candidates for the influential position of director general.

Europeans tout free market capitalism that looks out for people's social welfare; Asians back a Confucian form of state capitalism wherein government guides industry to a great extent; and Americans peddle "shock therapy" capitalism arrived at through unbridled deregulation. These systems can coexist, but it is wrong to expect them to mold into one, no matter how alluring this might be and no matter how much Americans revel in "winning" the Cold War. While Europeans may be curbing them to some extent, one cannot imagine them doing away with their social welfare programs, high wages, long-running unemployment benefits, and strict labor and environmental laws. The welfare culture of Western Europe will steer it away from American-style capitalism, and its liberal-minded and individualistic populations will certainly not adopt an Asian-style state-coordinated mercantilism. It would be equally naive to predict that Japan and the rest of East Asia will significantly shift their economic systems from those based on state capitalism and government guidance of industries to deregulated capitalism. Asian countries will budge little in their state-led pursuit of growth and export markets, especially in markets within the Asian region. No, the three systems will remain largely intact into the next century.

GATT and the rest of these agreements bring down tariffs, but they don't bring down cultural barriers. Local realities will remain even as nations form *pactos,* enter blocs, make unions, and become signatories of GATT. Because Brazil becomes a member of Mercosur (the free trade agreement between Brazil, Argentina, Uruguay, and Paraguay) and of GATT doesn't mean that foreigners won't have to learn how Brazilians operate and behave in order to be successful in business there.

In fact, noneconomic divisions between countries will only become deeper as competition intensifies. The most important of these is the gap between the world's rich and poor, but others will include the gulf between technology "haves" and "have-nots," between the resource-rich and resource-poor nations, and between those that have access to Western capital and those that do not. The dynamics of world demographics don't help. Ninety-five percent of the population increases between now and 2025 will occur in developing countries, among the world's poorest people.

We must avoid outmoded paradigms about how countries interconnect; each nation should be acknowledged for what it specifically has to offer. Peoples and nations may increase contact with one another in order to trade freely, but they prize their political and cultural independence now more than ever. This perspective on the world also accepts and acknowledges that America no longer occupies the center of the new world map, either culturally or economically.

How do we adopt a more universal perspective? One exercise is something we call "turning around the telescope." We get accustomed to looking at other countries, other peoples, and business opportunities through a telescope, zooming in to study details. In so doing, it's easy to lose sight of the forest for the trees. But try looking through the telescope from the other end, and one sees an entirely different picture. Instead of seeing the world divided into democracies and totalitarian regimes, or developed and undeveloped, or Global North and Global South, one sees the entire global picture. The paradigm here is to be able to shift from local reality to global reality, to zoom in and zoom out, to be able to look at opportunities in Cuba, but to dolly back and see how Cuba fits into the Carribean region, into Latin America, into the Americas, into the Western Hemisphere, into the world picture.

Making Your Global Net Work

Global firms are discovering the power of networks, relationships, and teamwork across national borders. "In the past," says futurist Alvin Toffler, "companies often mouthed the rhetoric of partnership. Today they are finding themselves thrust into it."[2] Olivetti, for example, has entered into 50 networking arrangements such as alliances, partnerships, agreements, and research and technology cooperation, says vice president for corporate economic research, Bruno Lamborghini. A firm's competitive position, he says, "will no longer depend solely on . . . internal resources," but on its network of relationships with outside companies and business units.[3]

As an international careerist, you will have to forge your own personal networks of connections with foreign businesspeople. Personal references matter more in foreign environments than they do in the United States. "If you are being considered for a new partnership," says Victor Fung, chairman of the Hong Kong investment bank Prudential Asia and a Chinese businessman well known overseas, "a personal reference from a respected member of the Chinese business community is worth more than any amount of money you could throw on the table."[4] Unfortunately for Westerners, personalized, in-group, commercial dealings are largely closed to strangers. "Many foreign enterprises," says author Shuji Hayashi, "expect instant membership in a club that has been closed for centuries."[5] World business networks can be based on family, ethnic group, or shared experience. Even the notorious Red Guards, who paraded "capitalist running dogs" through the streets during the Great Proletariat Cultural Revolution, now have formed a tight-knit business network in China.

Commercial relationships overseas are based on trust, sharing, partnership, loyalty, and respect rather than pure self-interest. The problem is compounded for Western newcomers, who often openly criticize local business practices and decry restrictions that seem inefficient and illogical, like the glacial slowness of decision making or an archaic distribution system. American businesspeople who are insensitive to local culture find themselves barred from vast networks of indigenous businesspeople.

In the United States, we don't depend so much on business linkage because we don't need to. Our system is step-oriented. There are rules and regulations that make up a clearly articulated procedure. You follow it and you succeed, more or less. In other business environments, predictable and accountable procedures may not exist. We must learn to prize linkage through relationships as much as the procedures.

For example, a large American company recently asked its subsidiary in Japan to conceive a marketing strategy for its products. The U.S. side imagined it would receive a report describing in sequence each recommended strategic move toward penetrating the Japan market. What it received was quite different—a one-page diagram depicting *relationships* between the subsidiary and two large Japanese companies that wielded a high degree of influence over a series of smaller companies that were potential buyers of the product. The thinking was that the U.S. company should forge links with the big guns and the smaller firms would obediently line up to buy. The "marketing strategy" was rendered as a series of circles connected by arrows of varying thicknesses representing the importance of the connections between firms, not the kind of linear step-by-step model one would expect a Western marketing firm to produce.

One can imagine an example of a Mexican or Filipino "marketing strategy," with circles representing key industrial families, or one from China, with its circles representing key ministries and government officials and lines representing direct and indirect *guanxi* (backdoor or informal) connections. Or for Indonesia, with

its circles representing key firms controlled by *bumiputera* (indigenous Indonesian-Malay) members of the president's immediate family. The point here is that business is tribal in much of the world,
based on bonds that the by-the-book Westerner normally fails to
understand.

Adopting a Global Approach to Your Career

Unskilled and technically illiterate Americans have already
learned that global technological integration doles out mixed bless-
ings; it might cost less to telephone Manila, but their jobs are
threatened by people in New Delhi. Jobs—whether skilled, blue
collar, or highly technical—cannot be protected in a global economy. America's unskilled laborers first felt the brunt of emerging
country low-cost labor in the 1970s and 1980s; now, even highly
trained software developers, among other white-collar workers in
the United States, see their competitive edge dulled and replaced
by toiling and teeming Third World laborers.

Whether you are a financial planner, architect, or photographer,
the first step in taking advantage of the global boom is to get
yourself out of a stay-at-home mindset. No matter what your profession, it's quite possible that global opportunities exist for you.
The demand overseas for such services as accounting, consulting,
and legal advice has soared.

As ironic as it sounds, you should think small. That is, enter
emerging markets thinking about ways to provide basic goods and
services to emerging peoples at a moderate price. Take Michael
Giles, for example. He's a 34-year-old Columbia Law graduate who
recently left his $160,000 a year job in Maryland as a marketer for
IBM to go to Soweto, where he found that only four laundromats
were serving the black township population of 4.5 million resi-
dents. He hit up the U.S. Overseas Private Investment Corporation
for a $9.3 million loan to start Quick-Wash-Dry Clean U.S.A.,

which then grew to a chain of coin-operated outlets now number-ing 108 throughout South Africa's black townships.[6]

Evaluate your educational goals. What are the new managers for the global era going to look like? They have to be less bureaucratic and more independent. They have to understand the priorities of other cultures, comprehend and appreciate the differences in econo-mies and political systems, and empathize with the motivations of people different from themselves. The new global managers are able to listen to people below them, and they know how to empower. They will be loyalty builders, team enthusiasts, rewarders, commu-nicators, hands-on types—and they won't be afraid to get under the machinery and get their fingernails dirty. To restructure companies and industries in the new economy, says Alvin Toffler, "is not a job for knit-picking, face-saving, bean-counting bureaucrats. It is, in fact, a job for individualists, radicals, gut-fighters, even eccentrics —business commandos, as it were, ready to storm any beach to seize power."[7]

You may want to think about how to reengineer your education to be less specialized. For example, in the banking industry, "the pure technologist is dead," says George P. DiNardo, chief technol-ogy officer for Citibank's Asian Consumer Business. "And so is the pure business person."[8]

Groom yourself for the international position by doing some head-hunting in reverse. Start by choosing the company you want to work for. Then study the countries it deals with and develop multicultural skills if necessary. Hit up smaller companies first, where you can gain crucial international experience. "Ex-pats now work more often for midsized companies, high-tech, fast-growing companies, rather than the traditional Fortune 500," says Jack An-derson of Ernst & Young Accountants in Paris.[9] In fact, American firms employing more than 500 people account for only 7 percent of U.S. exports, while one-half of U.S. exports are sold by compa-nies employing 19 or fewer people.

Broadening Your International Information Diet

Part of personally globalizing your perspective is feeding your mind with more globally oriented information. Read material from another perspective, like books about a country not written by an American. Read fiction from the culture of interest. Read about America in books and articles not written by Americans.

Subscribe to a magazine from another country, especially one about world events. Have a foreign student live with your family, or send your kid overseas as a student. Listen to the BBC on public radio. Travel more often to nontraditional destinations. Learn to read another language. Attend cultural arts classes. Watch *CNN World Report.* Or subscribe to a locally published newspaper or socially aware periodical from a region of interest.

When trying to learn about the potential of an emerging country, reading only business journalism can be misleading. Analyzing only statistics will lead you to false conclusions about the entrepreneurial tenacity and potential of a people and a country. Look at technical skills, tastes, needs, will, spirit, partnering potential, contentedness. Few economists predicted the East Asian takeoff; it was a *cultural* assessment that was the first empirical tool that helped to explain the region's economic boom. The so-called rational choice economic theory currently being touted in business schools as a crystal ball for predicting the growth potential of emerging nations wrongly admonishes its adherents to analyze only economic data of a subject country, and not the culture, temperament, and history of its people. Even Paul Kennedy in his classic treatise on country competitiveness, *The Rise and Fall of the Great Powers,* undervalues the role of ideology, religion, and culture.

"Irrational choices" open more interesting territory. Why do Chinese bureaucrats fear business risk as a potential loss of political clout, but readily accept a bribe? Why do Japan's best and brightest run the government while in the United States they flock to the private sector? Why is it said that the PRI (Institutional Revolutionary Party) government raids Mexico's treasury at the end of every six-year presidential term? Why does Taiwan seem so corrupt and Singapore so chaste? Why do the ethnic Chinese dominate the business communities of Thailand and Malaysia?

"You can't simply transfer our economic and political rules and institutions and make [developing nations] like us," says Robert Shoemaker at the African bureau of the Agency for International Development, who has applied a more "irrational" approach to helping poor nations move to market.[10] In assisting Cameroon he chose to tinker with the existing inefficient government-controlled local economy rather than attempt to impose a new market system.

When analyzing a host country's potential, also take into account cultural dynamism, incipient entrepreneurialism, distribution of computers, available databases, newspapers read, technical publications, research expertise, as well as the statistical facts and figures of the economy, including GNP and trade. Don't lean too much on statistics. Go to the place and observe. We might think that a country with no growth is a fallow land because such a statistic regarding the United States would imply as much. But an emerging country experiencing zero growth might signal genuine opportunity. Poland, for example, was hailed as a success in Eastern Europe when it achieved no growth, rather than continued negative growth due to the loss of its markets in the Soviet Union.

After you take a look at a target country through a wide-angle lens and compare it with others and with your own, zoom in for a close-up. What is the country doing compared to itself alone, judging from criteria calibrated to its own governmental, political, and social system? Only by using appropriate criteria will you be able to predict where the country is going.

Knowing Your Strengths and Minimizing Your Weaknesses

Adopting a global personality doesn't mean that you have to participate in ballooning races across China or the Pacific Ocean as have Malcolm Forbes and Richard Branson, respectively. But there is often a daredevil streak in the new globalist, a cocky willingness to prove that nothing is sacred. The new globalist is an adventurer. That doesn't mean you have to own an airline, but it does mean that you have to be willing (and able) to discover, act on gut instinct, go with a whim, and bounce back before your critics can mouth displeasure with you. Some of us have an easier time internationalizing our experience and perspective than others. Beyond the fact that some of us are just plain lazy, fear failure, fear the unknown, or are merely content with the status quo, going global has much to do with where one is coming from in terms of previous experience dealing with foreign places and people, as well as one's age, attitudes, and education.

Americans currently engaged with overseas counterparts can, in fact, be divided into groups. Depending on who you are, you can expect to encounter predictable obstacles and take with you certain strengths. The starting point for all of us is to recognize our inherent strengths and weaknesses, and to include as many positive features of each group as possible.

Old Guard Career Internationalists. The first-generation globalists who may have worked for a multinational firm in America's industrial heyday will likely possess business statesmanship and loads of overseas experience. They wield age seniority and possess connections, managerial know-how, savvy, and tangible technical knowledge based on years of hands-on work on specific projects (as opposed to the "vapor-expertise" of some college-trained graduates). However, while the Old Guard person may have seasoned experience, he or she may also have military experience in foreign countries that can get in the way, as well as attitudes about the might and right of America that might be outdated.

The B-School Globalists. The international MBAs who came into the job market in the 1980s have ample education, expertise, and connections, all of which makes them attractive to foreign partners. They may well share a similar school background with the educated English-speaking elite in a foreign country. People currently moving into higher-echelon business positions overseas match this group in age and in outlook. However, if they are too "me-oriented" (they did come of age in the eighties) they might find it hard to really appreciate another culture, and this can get in the way of connecting. They might, like Old Guards, be rugged individualists in approach overseas. Their extremely individualistic values (looking out for number one) may limit them when dealing with consensus-based cultures. Also, the majority of MBA programs offered during the 1980s were not international in orientation. Moreover, because the system of promotion in U.S. companies discourages taking international positions, these people can be rather cynical and short-term in perspective; they may be willing to relocate for a while, but from their point of view, the international posting may be a peril rather than a promotion, especially as they enter their forties.

Peace Corps Boomers and Culturists. Those who studied culture or sociology and perhaps worked a stint in the Peace Corps when young during the Kennedy years make good *friendship* connections overseas because they appreciate culture. Foreign businesspeople tend to be delighted when a culturist has a first meeting with them—the culturist can appreciate the foreigner's unique situation and wants to cooperate. And the culturist makes all the right promises. Unfortunately, most culturists don't wield the hustle power or business clout to come through on promises. They often lack the necessary business school connections, corporate network, and commercial acumen. Moreover, few Peace Corps boomers learned how to turn their knowledge of culture into a business that can really touch other people, although of the handful of viable U.S.-based international cross-cultural training businesses, some of the best are run by people with this background.

Generation X. Also known as twenty-somethings, Generation X-ers in many ways are more exposed to the world than any other groups. They're open to other cultures and are exposed to multiple cultural influences. They deify diversity, and if they have any literary and computer skills at all, they have instant access via the Internet to millions of people in virtually every country on the planet. Having grown up in a declining America, they are more likely to have considered alternative sites as the means to financial security.

Their global vision may be limited, though. They tend to believe that foreigners take on our cultural apparel because they admire its deeper aspects. Because they grew up in an America in decline, they perceive foreigners as being monied consumers of export products, from hamburgers to skateboards—that is, an easy market for American products, especially pop culture products. They often lack social skills, which can be an obstacle when dealing in other cultures more so than it is here. Also, because they tend to be entrenched in younger-aged pop culture, they can find it hard to forge relationships with foreign businesspeople who wield real power. They tend to have limited patience dealing with face-conscious and respect-sensitive cultures.

Employees of Foreign-Owned Companies in the West. These are people who may never have been abroad but have had a foreign culture imposed upon them. In their futures they may indeed be sent to the foreign city where the parent company is located. They perhaps have had to deal with a foreign manager or owner, and have probably hosted a foreign delegation from the parent company. They may have experience conducting negotiations with a foreign delegation, perhaps one representing the firm that has purchased the U.S. company.

Their possible disadvantage is that when you work for a subsidiary anywhere, whether a foreign subsidiary or a U.S. subsidiary, your affiliate is often treated like a stepchild by the parent company. When the parent is overseas, the employee may feel left out of the power loop, and may harbor a jaded view of the foreign party —and its culture. Often, foreign companies fire people after taking over subsidiaries and/or dismiss first those who don't share the cultural background of the new owners. On the other hand, these people may have been through cross-cultural team-building seminars, diversity training, and extended exposure to foreign business parties. They may have had the opportunity to connect with well-placed foreign people, and to learn cross-cultural communication skills.

Missionaries Across All Age Groups. Missionaries, especially those who really honor other cultures, have a tremendous advantage because they are trained in both language and culture. Devout Mormons spend two years doing missionary work overseas; large numbers of these people are in the U.S. workforce. For example, 80 percent of the employees at Evans & Sutherland, a flight simulator manufacturer in Utah, are former Mormon missionaries.

Ex-missionaries, however, may also carry with them a superior and condescending attitude toward other cultures. The possible weaknesses of a former-missionary-turned-international-business-person are that their overseas experience could be jaded by the fact they went abroad trying to *change* the local culture, to mold the "noble savage" in many cases. That does not an interculturalist make.

Import-Export Entrepreneurs. These people work in companies, or own companies, that buy from, or sell to, one or more foreign countries. They may have had personal dealings with foreign partners; they might have a production contract with a supplier in Bali or southern China or South Korea or Mexico. Out of their own initiative they have pursued overseas ties, and they are respected by foreign businesspeople, especially midlevel people and independent-minded trading people in the nonstate sector. There are tremendous numbers of people wanting to work with this kind of Westerner. They are under their own steam; they are not bound up in a constricting, plodding, corporate hierarchy, nor will they be fired next week. They wield instant and autonomous authority.

Their drawbacks might be that they have not had a superior to mentor them in the ways of doing business abroad. Mom-and-pop traders who get burned can become vehemently antiforeign. And they do get burned often because of their small size: a container-load of defective latex gloves may come from China, or their factory in Bali may sell to their U.S. competitor in breach of contract, or the amount of liquid in bottles imported from Mexico may be inconsistent. They have good low-level connections, but they tend to venture offshore not realizing that the local standard of business ethics simply may not match that in their own country. As a result, they often come away with jaded attitudes about dealing with foreign countries.

Envisioning Your Company's Path

After reading articles about globalism, one might grow to think that firms everywhere are packing their bags and expanding operations around the world en masse. Hardly. Globalization *is* taking place, but for most of the U.S. firms we talked to, it is individual business units of the firm that are going international, selling or setting up joint venture alliances overseas. International orientation is not part of the evolution of most American companies.

This is especially true with companies that have developed their international presence over time, with each overseas unit or venture existing in somewhat of a vacuum, far from home, and outside the purview of all other units of the firm except its board of directors. Rarely does umbrella oversight by a centralized CEO imbued with global vision take an entire firm global. An overall global strategy tying in all units of the firm is the rare exception rather than the rule. A strategy—whether in one's personal life or in business—

needs to rest on that mysterious catalyst to action called *vision*. We will speak more about a global corporate *strategy* in the last chapter; right now, you need to do three things to begin the process of building global vision within all echelons of your organization. (It doesn't matter whether you work in the mail room or an executive suite—vision can and should be shared by all.) Your first step is to envision your firm's path to globalization.

This process is best started by studying the broad development of your company's globalization. What stages has the company experienced in internationalizing? By understanding the past, one can more readily project global activities for the future.

Depending on the evolution and endeavors of your firm, its managers may be trying to centralize units that don't know each other, or decentralize units that have too long been under headquarter's thumb. The trouble is that there does not exist (not yet, anyway) a dehydrated management remedy you can just add water to and watch it solve the problem. "Think globally, but act locally" hardly embodies the tension that exists within firms attempting to simultaneously widen their global presence *and* enhance their responsiveness to local markets. Without a common management model for running the new Global Corporation, we are all on the starting line together. Still, the following models provide some lessons.

Matsushita Opts for Decentralization. Few companies have pursued decentralization as a corporate strategy as diligently as Matsushita, or so early in its evolution. The firm's various divisions —like Matsushita USA, Matsushita Europe, and Matsushita Asia— all operate with a great deal of autonomy. Says Ronn Richard, vice president of planning, technology, and public affairs of Matsushita Electric Corporation of America, "Each regional division operates independently in terms of its marketing, sales, personnel, and philanthropy, so these activities are in sync with local laws, customs, tastes, and business practices. Some of the firm's divisions and affiliated companies even make the same product and compete against each other in the international marketplace."

Isn't this a waste of resources and economy of scale, doing R&D, manufacturing, and marketing and sales activities in separate divisions? Mr. Richards admits, "The company does occasionally lose a little in terms of economy of scale. However, I firmly believe this loss is more than compensated for by the increased sense of competiveness, productivity, and efficiency that our divisional system creates. At Matsushita, competition begins at home, and it is this good-spirited internal competiveness that toughens us up from the start and allows us to compete aggressively and effectively against other firms in the marketplace. Indeed, if you look at all of the other large multinational corporations that have been run centrally, you will see that they are the ones that have been suffering the most in recent years."

But not so fast with all this autonomy giving.

Lest you think decentralizing overseas operations is the sole mode toward internationalizing, many large firms see their way to success through *centralizing*—enhancing synergies between independent units rather than emphasizing their autonomy. It often boils down to this: How do you get the plant in Nigeria to both know and care what the one in Brazil produces, and help introduce those products to its African customers when appropriate? Right now, among the majority of the most globalized U.S. firms, you can almost guarantee that the Nigerian unit will not know what the Brazilian unit is doing or anything about its product line. Cross talk and coordination are absent. Often, affiliates of the same company compete with other subsidiaries to such a degree that teaming them up to generate synergy is impossible; they're too busy focusing on outperforming one another.

Chevron Sees Benefits of Centralized Coordination. The requisites of the international marketplace—of global customers—may not be accepting of a small-is-beautiful approach, at least not yet. Take a look, for instance, at Chevron. "In certain countries," says manager of business development and consulting services John A. Haglund, "a coordinated effort becomes almost required vis-à-vis the culture of the country. For instance, in China, you're dealing with a strong government, and they want to think in terms of one [business] entity as opposed to fifteen different entities. Consequently, you will not be effective if you don't have some sort of coordinated approach."

To project a more unified face in China, Chevron started by designing a brochure for its Caltex joint venture. Says Haglund: "It's got the Chevron and Texaco logos on the front [with that of Caltex] and it's called The Power of Three." So the company goes into China as Caltex, but in presentations, meetings, and brochures, it packages itself as the mighty triumvirate. "That way," says Haglund, "the customer—which is really the combination of government bureaucracies, technocrats, and 'arms-length' buyers of products—has an understanding of the broad picture. The point is that the Chinese do not want to deal with a foreign company in an 'à la carte' manner." The same can be said of most emerging countries and their governments, especially on projects dealing with resource exploitation, agriculture, and infrastructure enhancement. The bigger—rather than the smaller—you are, the better.

Chevron and Matsushita are both good examples of multinational companies, one decentralized and one not. But what makes a company global is an integration of its resources across borders, as well as having foreign nationals on its board of directors and not just there as tokens. The global firm holds board meetings in different countries where strategic operations exist rather than just at the home headquarters. This, in fact, is a problem at Matsushita Corporation and it's why, in spite of Mr. Matsushita's global vision, the company sometimes alienates its foreign employees and executives, including Americans.

Teaming Up with Local Allies

The traditional corporate American view of global business was one of exploiting cheap labor and natural resources, aimed at serving a home market primarily. Many have set up overseas for reasons of lower cost, especially labor costs. Smith Corona, for example, saved $20 million annually by manufacturing in Mexico rather than Syracuse, New York (prior to the company filing for bankruptcy). Japan's approach also lacked an interdependent theme but, due to its lack of resources, was more "strategic" in its alliances with other countries.

The savvy strategist considers a whole spectrum of global imperatives other than "selling to a new market" or "exploiting cheap labor." The rising importance of time in manufacturing has slowed the rate of firms moving overseas merely to find cheap labor. In fact, labor has become a much smaller percentage of production costs, except of very simple goods. You might enter an equity joint venture with a strong local enterprise that has a ready market to serve, as well as the potential to supply mature markets from behind tariff barriers. General Electric has done this in Hungary. It has invested $100 million to buy a controlling interest in a company called Tungsram, with whom it is building a manufacturing platform to become GE's main supplier of products to all of Europe. Although Hungary's Tungsram has been selling lighting products only in Eastern Europe, GE looked at the deal as being an entryway into the European market as a whole. Motorola is following a shared R&D strategy in Asia by locating its new 326,000-square-foot Asia-Pacific headquarters in Hong Kong, called Silicon Harbour Centre. The enormous complex is not only the company's corporate headquarters, but also a design, manufacturing, and computer center serving the Asia region and employing highly trained technicians. The purpose of the strategy is not only to be nearer the region's fast-growing markets for semiconductor chips, but also to utilize the talents of Chinese technical people.

For firms that have no presence in a burgeoning market, *licensing* may be a way to participate there. It's one example of a key strategy: namely, to team up with local allies. Find a strong upstart partner like the one Wal-Mart has linked up with—the famed ethnic Chinese conglomerate from Thailand, the Charoen Pokphand Group—with whom it will open stores in China and Hong Kong. The Thai group has already signed 55 ventures in the People's Republic of China and is said to be the largest foreign investor in the country, placing more capital there than Volkswagen, Pepsico, or Golden Wu, the Hong Kong entrepreneur who has put over $1.5 billion into the PRC. "There's not a heck of a lot that we know about retailing in China," says Don Shinkle, Wal-Mart's vice president for corporate affairs, "so we found an outstanding teacher."[11] Charoen Pokphand is hardly interested in pursuing only "core competencies." Rather, it is keen on achieving speed and connection making. Already, its dispersed endeavors include those in agribusiness, petrochemicals, property development, and manufacturing. The company is diverse, secretive, and family run.

Toshiba Corporation started building alliances with foreign companies in the early 1900s, starting with an agreement with General Electric to make light-bulb filaments. It now boasts partnerships with firms such as Apple Computer, Ericsson, Motorola, Olivetti, and Samsung. Fumio Sato, Toshiba's president and chief executive, explains: "It is no longer an era in which a single company can dominate any technology or business by itself. The technology has become so advanced, and the market so complex, that you simply can't expect to be the best at the whole process any longer."[12] In his opinion, the only way to keep up in the high-tech wars ahead is to choose the right partners who can pool innovation and resources.

Qualifying partners may be the most critical part of doing global deals—especially in emerging countries filled with instant entrepreneurs toting briefcases full of joint venture contracts. "Finding the right partner regardless of nationality is the key to future global success," says Uniden chairman Yoshio Sakai.[13]

Diversifying—Not Standardizing—Drives Expansion

The late 1980s saw the failure of global selling strategies first put forward by marketing guru Theodore Levitt of Harvard. "[T]he world's needs and desires have been irrevocably homogenized," Levitt said. Firms, he claimed, could now advertise and sell standardized mass-produced products all over the world as well as at home. The problem is that the world's markets differ in taste and preference, and the distinctiveness does not seem to be evaporating.

A truly "global" company or product line is simply an unrealizable fantasy in the majority of cases. Adaptation of approach, strategy, and specifications is almost always necessary. And consumer tastes are becoming more diverse. Even Americans now eat sushi, tacos, Thai food, and other foreign foods while continuing to eat hamburgers and apple pie. Says trendmeister John Naisbitt: "The more choice, the more discrimination in choice, and the more appetite for additional options. The more we integrate, the more we differentiate."[14]

Consider that the Japanese computer software industry is dominated by operating systems that are incompatible with DOS or Macintosh. Or how media titan Rupert Murdoch learned an expensive lesson about the divergent tastes of Asian television viewers; his STAR cable broadcasts have had to be customized for virtually every country of the region (cricket for Indonesians, sentimental Chinese music videos for Taiwanese, and so on).

Look for ways to standardize components but remain willing to adapt final products to local needs and preferences. Cost-cutting standardization is the objective, but the Coca-Cola recipe, for example, is changed for some countries and McDonald's hamburgers come with peppers in restaurants along the U.S.-Mexican border.

Understanding the Real Priorities of Partner Nations

A global corporate vision must include a will to help people in developing countries help themselves by teaching them the skills they lack. In these countries, practice the art of helping your partners achieve their own solutions rather than insisting that they implement yours. Too many Western companies try to stuff Western-style solutions down the throats of emerging countries, which is self-defeating. Third World countries have problems that need Third World solutions, not Western solutions.

Russia, for example, though not a Third World country, is not a country with a mercantile history. The country was isolated from the capitalist West for decades. The concept of competitive commerce is new to them. They are learning it, but at the same time you have to realize that Russia is in the same situation that Germany was in during the pre-Nazi Weimar Republic: severe economic problems, a population that needs its self-esteem pumped up, a turbulent political situation. A Westerner tends to offend the locals by offering ready-made Western-style answers to what are uniquely Russian problems. "You find that Russians are resistant to that," says Russia specialist Barbara Chronowski. "Westerners should not be telling the Russians what to do in the way that they are, even if what they're telling them is a perfect solution. *It's how we're saying it.* You may know business, they say, but you don't know Russia. You don't understand what our reality is."

Your firm needs to see itself working like a sort of economic development therapist in the Third World. It needs to say that it understands the locals' reality and wants to listen rather than instruct. Ask what you can do to help them rather than just analyze their problems and give them your solution. Many American firms are not being culturally sensitive to indigenous realities.

The corporate mantras for the next century are *teamwork, synergy,* and *partnership.* The notion of win/win will come of age as the era of imperialistic exploitation comes under mounting public outcry and organized pressure. You might have to reinvent your vocabulary and adjust your mentality, putting emphasis on mutual benefits, if not humanitarianism, in your business endeavors overseas. Cronyism and good-old-boy networks of stodgy monopolists are being replaced by alliances between partners who each possess a component in the formula for success. A global firm must put in place the people and the organizations to facilitate the sort of linkage and coordination and knowledge sharing that makes such an approach possible.

So, too, a purely electronic interface is no match for a sensitive, patient, and culturally knowledgeable person on the ground. With all of the hype about the Information Superhighway, a word of warning is warranted: Internet communications may not facilitate the global interpersonal communication necessary for forging personal commercial links overseas. In fact, electronic communication might even encourage isolationism—a way of extending your list of contacts without growing a real network of influential people who are willing to actively support your business interests. Electronic relationships, by definition, lack human contact; it's easier to burn a partner in business whom you know only through electronic connection. In this age in which ethnic groups and communities are reclaiming their identities and feeling the loss of roots and community, connection is clearly paramount in commerce.

Toward the turn of the century, we will see money digitized, shopping taking place at the virtual mall, and an increasing amount of advertising and business communication taking place on the Internet. For those Third World countries that have access to information technology and the skills to market their goods and services electronically, the cyber-marketplace will allow them access to customers they would otherwise have no hope of reaching. In the meantime, however, we can't overlook the power of personal connection. A corporate global view envisions the future while minding the present: fewer than four Americans per 1,000 are reachable on the Internet. Around the world, only 20,000 firms and 30 million people are on the Internet (although their numbers are rising by over 10 percent a month). Of the 600 million telephones in the world, 450 million are located in only *nine* countries.

Global Internet hucksterism is part of a brave new world to be. For now, heed the advice of a sage, anonymous salesman: "Nothing happens unless you're there in person." Americans abroad are often considered impersonal in business style, insensitive to local cultures, and impatient with foreign business practices. If anything, Americans need to become more personally involved in their overseas business dealings.

The following quiz will help you gauge your level of global vision, and that of your company. Similar questionnaires will appear in all the chapters that follow. Each of the two segments below has a possible 50 points. If you or your company scores below 25, you might want to concentrate your energies on upgrading your global vision, and that of your firm.

Part I: Assessing Yourself for Global Vision

Answer each item by circling the appropriate number on the continuum below:

To Almost No Extent		To Some Extent		To a Great Extent		To a Very Great Extent			
1	2	3	4	5	6	7	8	9	10

I make an effort to focus on my job at hand while also seeing how it relates to trends generated by economic globalization.

1   2   3   4   5   6   7   8   9   10

I am trying to build my own personal network of contacts and friendships around the world.

1   2   3   4   5   6   7   8   9   10

I consciously try to include sources of international news and business information in my "information diet," in the forms of watching certain television broadcasts, subscribing to certain periodicals and on-line services, etc.

1   2   3   4   5   6   7   8   9   10

I understand how my job function is going to change in the near future because of internationalization, and have prepared plans.

1   2   3   4   5   6   7   8   9   10

I keep abreast of how my firm is responding to globalization and try to contribute to that process in any way that I can.

1   2   3   4   5   6   7   8   9   10

Part II: Assessing Your Company for Global Vision

My work group or division has created a clearly articulated plan for its international business activities.

1   2   3   4   5   6   7   8   9   10

My division or work group monitors and responds to changes in the international market.

1   2   3   4   5   6   7   8   9   10

My company considers options in other countries other than selling to them directly or utilizing their inexpensive labor.

1   2   3   4   5   6   7   8   9   10

My firm actively seeks to form partnerships and alliances with overseas companies.

1   2   3   4   5   6   7   8   9   10

My company takes the time to acknowledge and respond to the unique needs of its foreign customers, which are expected to be different from those of our domestic customers.

1   2   3   4   5   6   7   8   9   10

STRATEGY II
Developing Cultural Empathy

As the world economy becomes increasingly integrated, we seem to assume that along with it a universal "international business culture" is taking root around the world. This, however, is not really the case. While consumer trends and tastes around the globe have become more standardized and far-reaching, the internationalization of consumer culture has triggered an opposing trend: the retrenchment of individuals into the comfort zone of their unique cultures.

The economic dominance of the United States has given us global visibility and an economically central position, but in many ways our influence, especially in the area of business culture, has been misleading and seriously overestimated. It has caused many Americans to assume that the trend in world cultures is toward universalization of American business practice. We tend to think of other countries as Americas-in-the-making, naturally wanting to imitate and adopt our cultural traits, values, and priorities. However, other cultures tend to imitate ours more as a fashion statement than as a commitment. A deep synthesis of our culture into theirs is simply not happening.

The rest of the world does not necessarily want to emulate us. In fact, many nations have serious reservations about opening their cultural borders to the influence of American media, business practices, and social behavior. The fact is, American culture is rejected as often as it is accepted in the new order. The Philippines, for example, insisted on the removal of the U.S. military bases from their soil to resist further cultural corruption, although it meant suffering tremendous financial loss.

Many leaders in Asian and Middle Eastern countries see Western culture as contaminating their youth. While the older generation tries to preserve tradition, the younger generation eagerly embraces American pop culture—from Mickey Mouse to Michael Jackson—as a sign of being "in." Although there is no evidence that the youth throughout the world are becoming more like each other in real terms, the older generation often sees these superficial preferences as a threat to deeper values.

Even within Western nations, there are often concerted efforts to avoid being "corrupted" by other cultures. The French, for example, have fought the use of English words tooth and nail, going so far as to publish "official translations" of fashionable foreign words in "real" French and mandating that public officials use these rather than the popular "Franglais" versions of the words. At GATT talks they cited the corrupting effects of American culture as the reason for maintaining barriers to the wholesale import of U.S. films.

Rather than homogenize them or cause their extinction, modern technology has given indigenous ethnic groups like the Thule Indians of North America, the Aymara of South America, the Taureg of North Africa, the Faeroos of Western Europe, and the Abkhaz of the Russian continent the power to claim their right to self-determination and preserve their traditional culture more so than ever. Though the Thais and the Hmong and the Hui may listen to Madonna, this has not meant that they don't use their tape cassette recorders to archive their own folk songs, stories, and voices. In fact, Jack Weatherford in his recent book *Savages and Civilization* underscores that the spread of technology around the planet has resulted in a great blossoming of human cultural diversity rather than its predicted homogenization into a Hollywoodized hybrid called World Culture.

The West is fractured culturally too. Joel Garreau's *The Nine Nations of North America* divides that region into nine separate and distinct cultural enclaves. The European continent can be divided into such cultural islands as well, says the brewery baron Freddie

Heineken of Holland. And not into just 9, but 75 "countries," each with a population of 5 to 10 million people who share a similar ethnic and historic background.

Your global vision should include room for all of the world's 500 large-population ethnic groups. Sophisticated foreign business elites may speak English and receive their college degrees in the West, but to reach the common people anywhere, a global company will have to know the local customs and business practices. The growth of diaspora populations is another trend to include in one's global vision; 50 million Chinese, 7 million Jews, 5 million Indians (the list goes on) now live outside their homelands.

Too often our firms go global but remain parochial and ethnocentric, attitudes that can lead to commercial impotence. Part of the problem is that the American boardroom is still made up primarily of white males of European ancestry: a kind of old-boy network entrenched in the perspective of American invincibility and superiority—a throwback to the heady postwar era. Minorities, who could supply alternative, and more international, perspectives, remain strikingly outnumbered.

The American value system may, in some ways, alienate us from much of the rest of the world. On many accounts, we could, in fact, be called the "oddball" culture of the world rather than the common ground. There may be comfort in doing business only with culturally similar people, but such an attitude (though perhaps part of human nature) is clearly unprogressive. "The challenge now facing us," says Jack Weatherford, "is to live in harmony without living in uniformity, to be united by some forces such as world commerce, pop culture, and communications, but to remain peacefully different in other areas such as religion and ethnicity."

As an exercise in acknowledging the diversity of your world customer base, try to imagine a world in which every world ethnic group obtains self-rule inside its own independent country. Here's what just a *partial* list might look like.

Examples of Cultural Groups of the World

North America

Aleuts	Cuna	Northwest Indians
Ammassasalimiut	Dakota	Objibwa
Anthapaskins	Garifuna	Papagos/Pimas
Apaches	Great Basin Indians	Plateau Indians
California Indians	Huastee	Pueblos
Cheyenne	Inupik (Eskimo)	Thule
Cree	Iroquois	Yupik (Eskimo)
Creek	Navajos	Zuni

Central America

Carib	Mestizos	Tarahumara
Caribbean Blacks	Mixtecs	Totonacs
Creoles	Mopan Maya	Tzotzil
Huichol	Mulattos	Yaqui
Maya	Nahua	Zapota

South America

Aymara	Guambiano	Otavalo
Campa	Guarani	Quechua
"Chubut Patagonian Welsh"	Jivaro	Quillacinga/Pasto
	Mapuche	Vaupe's Indians
Chulupi	Mataco	Warrau
"Favelados" (Shanty-town dwellers)	"Nordrestinos"	Yanomamo

North Africa

Baggara	Kababish	Sanike
Berbers	Katyle	Taureg
Copts	Moors	Teda
Fulani	Nafusa	Toucouleur
Homr	Reguibat	Wolof
Ja'aliyyin		

Sub-Saharan Africa

Acholi	Ashanti	Boers
Afars	Bafut	Bushmen
Amhara	Bamilake	Chokwe
Asante	Bemba	Dan

Dinka
Dogon
Ewe
Fang
Fon
Fulbe
Ganda
Gonja
Hausa
Herero
Hutu
Ibo
Issas
Kamba

Kavengo
Kikuyu
Kipsigis
Konga
Kwangu-Kwilu
Masai
Mende
Merina
Ndebele
Nuer
Ovambo
Ovimbundu
Pygmies

Rotse
Shilluk
Shona
Somali
Sotho
Swahili
Swazis
Tswana
Tutsi
Xhosa
Yoruba
Zande
Zulus

West Europe

Alsatians
Andalusians
Basques
Catalans
Celts
Corsicans
Danes
English
Faeroos

Finns
Flemish
French
Galicians
Germans
Icelanders
Irish
Italians
Lapps/Samer

Norwegians
Portuguese
Sards
Scottish Gaels
Sicilians
Spaniards
Swedes
Swiss
Welsh

East-Central Europe

Albanians
Bosnian Muslims
Bulgarians
Cretans
Croatians
Czechs
Estonians

Greeks
Gypsies
Hungarians
Latvians
Lithuanians
Macedonians
Moldavians

Montenegrins
Poles
Romanians
Serbians
Slovaks
Slovenians

The Russian Continent

Abkhaz
Armenians
Azerbaijanis
Bashkir
Buryat
Chechen
Cherkess

Chukchee
Cossacks
Daghestanis
Evenki
Georgians
Kalmuk
Karelians

Khanti
Komi
Koryak
Mansi
Mari
Nanai
Nentsi

Osset	Tatars	Ukranians
Russians	Tuva	Yakuts

The Middle East

Alawites	Ibodi	Muscati
Arabians (Gulf)	Iranians	Omani
Arabians (Saudi)	Iraquis	Palestinians
Arads	Jews	Qashqai
Bakhtiari	Jordanians	Shahscvan
Baluch	Kurds	Syrians
Bedouin	Lebanese	Turks
Druze	Marsh Arabs/Ma'dan	Yemenites

Central Asia

Apa Tanis	Gujarati	Nepalese
Badagas	Hazara	Newars
Baigas	Hill Marias	Nishi
Bengalis	Ho	Nuristani
Bhils	Irulars	Oraons
Bhotias	Jains	Parsi
Borusho	Jats	Pashtun
Chakar Aimeq	Kachari	Pundits/Bhotta
Chencha	Karava	Santals
Daflas	Khalka	Sherpas
Drukpa	Khasi	Sikhs
Durrani	Khonds	Sinhalese
Gadabas	Konda Raddis	Tamils
Garo	Lepcha	Tibetans
Garungs	Munda	Yanadi
Gonds	Nagas	

East Asia

Ainu	Jinuo	Mongols
Amoy	Kaoshan	Pai
Hakka	Koreans	Tibetans
Han	Manchus	Uighurs
Hui-hui	Miao	Yao
Japanese	Min-chia	

Southeast Asia

Abelam	Anga	Asmat
Achinese	Apayao	Bagobo
Akha	Arapesh	Bajau

Balinese	Ilocano	Pangasinan
Batak	Jakun	Rejang
Bicolano	Jale	Sagada Igorot
Bontoc Igorot	Javanese	Samal
Buginese	Kachin	Sangir
Bukidnon	Kalinga	Sapik River People
Burmese	Karen	Shan
Cebuano	Khmer	Subanon
Cham	Lao	Sundanese
Chin	Lisu	Tagalog
Dani	Madurese	Tai
Dayak	Makasarese	Tasaday
Dusun	Malay	Tau Sug
Filipinos	Maluccans	Temiar
Fore	Mangyan	Thai
Gajo	Manus	Tinggian
Goilala	Melpa	Tolai
Hiligaynon	Menangkabau	Toradja
Hmong/Mao	Minangkabau	Wa
Huli	Mon	Waray-waray
Iban	Moros	Vietnamese
Ifugao	Pampangan	Yakan

Oceania (including Australia, New Zealand, and the Pacific Islands)

Australian Aborigines	Maori	Samoans
Dobuans	Melanesians	Tahitians
Fijians	Micronesians	Tongans
Hawaiians	Polynesians	

Culture Clashes

Culture-based conflicts happen all the time in the present-day global business environment. Corning's joint venture in Mexico, for instance, suffered a complete undoing because of culture-based problems. On June 26, 1994, the *New York Times* reported on the collapse of the 25-month-old $130 million joint venture between Corning, the giant U.S. ceramic cookware manufacturer, and Vitro, an enormous Mexican glass manufacturer. The prospects for compatibility had looked extremely promising since the two companies had important similarities and objectives. Both were international in scope but still family controlled, and both had a consumer-oriented philosophy with a long list of successful joint ventures. All who were interviewed about the breakup attributed the expensive and disappointing outcome to constant culture clashes.

To begin with, critical decisions about marketing and sales were continually delayed, because in the Mexican culture only top management, which was always busy with other issues, can make them. When it came to sales discussions, Vitro favored the less aggressive Mexican approach. Attempts to schedule meetings between their respective bankers to work up a consumer credit card became a comedy: the Americans wanted to work through lunch for a straight eight-hour day, while the Mexicans would take hours for lunch, coming back late in the afternoon expecting an evening meeting, which might last until nine at night. The Mexican managers saw the Americans as too direct, too impatient, and disinclined to admit fault. The American managers saw the Mexicans as too polite and too slow.

The Americans wanted rational, linear decisions, whereas the Mexicans wanted to consider other issues such as relationships, traditions, and personal loyalties, and often reached their decisions by consensus, in a "gentlemanly" way. The Americans had no problem with criticizing or laying blame on a person, while the Mexicans preferred to focus on the positive aspects of the partnership. In Mexico, contracts are not necessarily viewed as "law" but as goals, resulting in endless financial problems. Remembering to use titles and the bountiful honorifics was crucial, but vexing for the Americans. For the Mexicans extending a weekend to encompass Monday and a national holiday on Tuesday was commonplace. From Corning's ultramodern headquarters in upstate New York to Vitro's ornate sixteenth-century-style office building in Monterrey, the misunderstandings are bound to result in career casualties.

Sometimes, the problem is simply a lack of cultural awareness. A case in point was the San Diego Soviet Arts Festival held in 1989. The visitors were performers from both Georgia and Russia. The organizers made the mistake of being insensitive to nationality. In fact, when the festival was first conceived, it had been named the *Russian* Arts Festival. The Georgians were deeply offended because the word "Russian" implied the Russian nationality, to the exclusion of the Georgian. To make matters worse, the Americans on the mayor's committee organizing the festival continued to refer to the visiting members of the delegations from the Soviet Union as "Russians," whether or not the people they were speaking to were Ukrainian, Georgian, or Russian. When Georgian folk dancers arrived, they saw that the festival was being billed as a "Russian" festival, and requested to be put back on their plane and taken back to Georgia. They would not even sit with the Russians at banquets, or talk to them. "San Diego would like to say that the festival was a success," says a Russia expert who worked with the event's organizers, "but in terms of interaction between the Americans and the different Soviet nationalities, it was not so good."

Other clashes occur when people are simply behaving in an ethnocentric or insensitive manner. An American marketer working for Science Applications International Corporation on a $10 million sale of equipment to the Chinese, asked representatives of the Chinese buying enterprise—which employs 10,000 people—if it planned to pay "with rice, or what?" Not long ago another American visiting Eastern Germany was asked by his host, during polite conversation, if he had ever seen Berlin before. The American replied: "Only from the air, when we bombed it during the war."

These problems point to the need for our representatives to increase their cultural awareness and empathy for other cultures. We have two objectives before us. First, to build cross-cultural awareness and skills in ourselves; and second, to build into your firm's corporate culture an emphasis on cross-cultural adaptability and cultural sensitivity training.

What happened at Corning-Vitro was certainly a culture clash, beginning with a fundamental clash of cultural values. Values are the foundation on which we structure our lives, the basic beliefs from which we formulate guidelines for behavior. Values and assumptions greatly affect our belief systems, which are usually deeply ingrained and include opinions on things like religion, divorce, abortion, race, human rights, sex, equality, punishment, environmental issues, political systems, and poverty. We tend to be drawn to people who share our beliefs, and many people feel threatened by those who have different or opposing beliefs. Our values, assumptions, and belief systems determine the way we perceive phenomena. No action or event has meaning in and of itself. Meaning must be assigned to it, and our values and beliefs govern what meaning we will ascribe.

The Mexicans at Vitro, for example, valued strong interpersonal relationships, human dignity, and enjoying life as you live it. Their behavior was thus characterized by consideration of people's "face" and personal loyalties; polite, respectful speech; and the tendency to take long breaks during the workday. The Americans at Corning, on the other hand, valued aggressively attacking problems, egalitarian conduct, and accomplishing tasks. Their propensity for openly criticizing individuals, their difficulty with titles, and their desire to work straight through the day to complete their goals reflected this. The cultural assumptions by both Corning and Vitro interfered with their ability to realize, before it was too late, that the other side had a different, but valid, approach. Each side made assumptions about concepts of time, relationships, truth, reality, and the nature of humankind. Thus the Mexicans perceived the Americans as too direct and impatient, whereas the Americans saw the Mexicans as too polite and too slow. Both sides were judging the actions and behaviors of the other against the standards of their own culture.

Ethnocentrism

Ethnocentrism is the attitude that your culture is intrinsically superior to others, and that its way is the right way. From this perspective, another culture's customs may seem silly, bizarre, ab-surd, or even immoral. But, in fact, there is no absolute universal code with which one can judge cultural customs. What is right, wrong, good, or bad are relative concepts, dependent on the values of that culture. This "cultural relativism" means that when assess-ing the actions of people from another culture, it is imperative to look at their behavior in terms of that culture's norms and values—in other words, in its cultural context. Putting one's own culture at the center of the universe is a natural tendency; it's the most basic method a culture has of validating itself. When working with peo-ple from other cultures, however, this sense of superiority and self-righteousness leads to severe cultural myopia, and consequently, to resentment from the other side.

Sometimes even well-intentioned acts may spring from ethno-centric views and thus may not be received with the enthusiasm expected by the initiator. Our history is replete with such deeds. In 1744, the government of Virginia informed the Indians of the Six Nations in a speech at Lancaster, in Pennsylvania, that there was a college at Williamsburg with a fund for educating Indian youth. The government of Virginia further declared that if the chiefs of the Six Nations would send half a dozen of their sons to that college, the government would take care that they be well provided for and instructed in all the learning of white people. The Indians were nonplussed. Some of their sons had been educated by Whites in the past. Benjamin Franklin reported the rest of the Indian spokesman's reply in his pamphlet *Remarks Concerning the Savage North America,* published in 1784:

> [S]everal of our young people were formerly brought up at the Colleges of the Northern Provinces; they were in-structed in all your science; but when they came back to us they were bad runners, ignorant of every means of living in the woods, unable to bear either cold or hunger, knew nei-ther how to build a cabin, take a deer, nor kill an enemy,

spoke our language imperfectly . . . [they] were therefore fit neither for hunters, warriors, nor counsellors; they were totally good for nothing. [I]f the gentlemen of Virginia will send us a dozen of their sons, we will take care of their education, instruct them in all we know and make Men of them.

Not only does ethnocentrism generate a superior and self-righteous point of view, but it also often leads to selective or false portrayals of history, invariably with your culture cast as the "good guy." Antoine Morrison, an American consultant with Loaiza, Morrison, Peña Asociados Mexico, was helping a Texas company sell its products to the Mexican government. As the Mexican officials were driving along the Avenida Reforma in Mexico City with the American executives from Texas, they passed a huge statue. One of the officials turned to Morrison and asked him to tell their guests from Texas about the history of the statue. Morrison sensed trouble, but told the Texans that the statue was dedicated to the Niños Heroes, or Heroic Children, who died in 1847 defending their military college against U.S. troops who had invaded Mexico City. When the brief battle was over, the school was destroyed and all the cadets were dead. One of the cadets, Juan Escutia, wrapped himself in the Mexican flag to prevent its capture and flung himself to the rocks below. Throughout Mexico, streets, schools, libraries, parks, and hospitals bear the name "Niños Heroes," and the five-peso note carries their portraits. Suddenly, one of the Americans drawled: "The U.S. Army invading Mexico City? That's pure bullshit!" Morrison lamented later, "If only the Texan had responded with a simple neutral-sounding 'What a tragic event,' the business could have been saved."

When we meet someone from a foreign culture, it's like two icebergs running into each other. As we know, only about 10 percent of an iceberg is visible above water; the bulk of it lies submerged. In the iceberg model, behaviors, words, customs, and traditions would exist above the surface, while assumptions, values, beliefs, perceptions, and thoughts reside below, unseen. The part of us that exists above the surface is easy to see but difficult to interpret without a deeper understanding. If we're not aware of our extensive invisible substructure, we are more prone to causing cultural collisions without even knowing it. We may move about bombarding others with values we aren't even fully aware we own.

Take a minute to consider, first, what a typical American iceberg would look like if you actually wrote out some of these customs, behaviors, assumptions, values, and beliefs. Next, consider what your own personal iceberg might look like. It's important to be aware of how influenced by our cultures each of us is and how we differ from our cultural influences.

Stereotyping

Generalizations are not necessarily evil. They allow us to draw a sort of road map. The important thing to remember is that it is not a very detailed map; they represent a *general* map. And equally important is to remember not to turn these into rigid preconceptions of individuals.

People tend to use new experience as evidence to support their foregone conclusions. For example, if the Americans at Corning had a prejudged opinion of Mexicans as lazy, then they would be tempted to view the lunch hour behavior of the bankers as confirmation of Mexican laziness, rather than as a custom (a common one in hot climates). If the Mexicans at Vitro already had a stereotype of Americans as impatient, then they would be likely to view the Corning team's behavior as impatient, rather than dedication to getting the job done.

Just as you might carry around conscious and subconscious stereotypes of others, your foreign partners, also, probably do the same about you. Perceptions of Americans vary, depending on who's doing the looking—or stereotyping. The two lists below reveal frequent cultural stereotypes of Americans. While Asians tend to see us more like the left-hand column, Latin Americans see us more like the right.

IDEALISTIC	REALISTIC
INDIVIDUALISTIC	TEAM-ORIENTED
EASYGOING	ALWAYS IN A HURRY
EMOTIONAL	UNEMOTIONAL
EXTROVERTED	RESERVED
JOKERS	SERIOUS
SELF-INDULGENT	SELF-DISCIPLINED
PRODUCTION-ORIENTED	QUALITY-CONSCIOUS

Stereotypes, though based on elements of truth, are exaggerations. As you look at the following list of stereotypes of U.S. businesspeople, consider whether or not you fit any of them.

EXTRAVAGANT

LOUD

RUDE

WASTEFUL

WEALTHY

BOASTFUL

IMPATIENT

IMMATURE

Most of us feel we do not fit these stereotypes, even if we know others who do. A norm is only valid when applied to a group of people, not to individuals. *Everyone* would feel that in some way she or he varies from the norm. It is therefore important to find out the ways that the individuals you are working with do not fit the norms of their culture.

When you consider what is at stake in these cross-cultural encounters (fortunes, reputations, jobs, to name a few), leaving things to chance seems like a passport to failure. Here are some tips to help you become more comfortable in the new global theater and avoid ethnocentrism and rigid or prejudiced stereotyping.

Get to know yourself above and below the surface. Know your own "cultural luggage," that is, your values and assumptions that determine what you believe to be proper. These will largely determine how you perceive (and subsequently judge and stereotype) people with a different set of luggage. Being clear on who you are, and what part of you is a product of your culture, is the first step in crossing cultures gracefully and effectively. Examine your values and their origins. Look at them objectively.

Foster a sense of humility and respect for others. Learn how to laugh at yourself and to admit you don't know when you don't. People don't expect you to know everything about their culture, but they expect you to *want* to know. Find your sense of humor, as well as your sense of savvy. Develop a positive attitude toward feedback, rather than seeing it as criticism, since this may be the only gauge you'll have for the successfulness of your efforts to adapt. Learn how to hold your tongue when your opinion is not asked or may not be well received. There is not universal respect for "speaking your mind."

Show respect for the other's values. When a value system runs counter to yours, it is essential that you respect others' right to their beliefs. You must resist displaying a conviction that yours is superior. Being ethnocentric inspires the same destructive attitude in the other person; it's a natural defensive response. When confronted by unusual behavior, try to identify what motivates it. By ascertaining what values are coming into play, you will be better equipped both to understand the logic behind the action and to predict subsequent behavior.

Develop a tolerance for contradiction and ambiguity. Every culture has contradictions, including our own. We're so used to ours that we hardly notice them. But in new surroundings contradictions may stand out like a sore thumb. In the Asian yin-yang concept, it's the contrasting opposites that make life complete. Acceptance is advised.

In addition, there may be many occasions when you haven't a clue as to what's going on in your new environment, so cultivate the ability to be comfortable in ambiguous and unfamiliar situations. Try to just "go with the flow" without having to control, interpret, or understand it at the moment. There will usually be opportunities at a later time to ask questions or reanalyze things when more data is available.

Withhold judgment while observing. When you meet people and do not know anything about their beliefs and values, observe their actions and listen to their words without passing judgment. There is a critical difference between observing (which is neutral) and judging, and you need to learn to excel in the former. Let's say you walk into someone's office, and while you're talking with him, he continues to lean back in his chair with his feet on his desk. A correct observation, without value judgment, is simply that he is leaning back in his chair with his feet on his desk. Judgments are often conclusions drawn on assumptions rather than facts. If this took place in a culture where that behavior is expected, or if there were some other extenuating circumstance (his doctor had given him strict orders to do so), then judging him as rude, informal, or disrespectful would be incorrect. If you understand a behavior to be a cultural custom, you must also realize that, whether or not you like that behavior, it has cultural integrity.

Elements of Culture

Preparing to enter another culture is critical. The following are some of the elements you should learn about before entering another culture.

Ethnic Background. Few countries are monoethnic. The United States is a prime example. The norms of Jews, Italians, Blacks, and various Asian groups differ significantly. While all children growing up in this country are inculcated with "traditional American values," many will also acquire the norms of their ethnic group. When working with people from another country, it is critical to understand the influences of a person's ethnic background. The Malaysian of Chinese heritage, for example, differ greatly from their Muslim countrymen.

Class. Many countries have a clear class system, with different professions associated with different groups. Higher education may be available only to certain groups. Often, different behavior is expected from those of a higher social class than from those of a lower one, so it's vital to know where your counterpart fits into the hierarchical system. It is also important that you, too, in some ways, live up to the expectations of your status. People in hierarchical systems are often most comfortable when people exhibit behavior reflective of their position.

Regional Differences. Even in small countries, regional differences can be significant. Let's take Spain, a country larger than California but smaller than Texas, which has four official languages: Castilian, Catalán, Basque, and Galician, with Castilian being the one most Americans are familiar with. The other three languages are widely spoken in Spain, and there are polemical discussions in several other regions (Asturias and Aragon) to promote their dialects to the status of languages. Regional differences are constantly discussed in Spain, causing one visitor to draw the conclusion that "there are perhaps no Spaniards, only Gallegos, Andaluces, Salamantinos, Catalanes, Madrileños and so on." People from Madrid may consider those coming from Asturias as "immigrants," as might Barcelonians consider those from Andalucia.

Individual Differences. Many factors can contribute to individual differences. These include age, education, upbringing, gender, position, exposure to foreign cultures, individual personality, past experiences, and so on. Some individuals' personalities are naturally so different from the style of the culture they were born into that they never really feel as if they fit in. Indeed, for some it is only when they travel to a culture more in sync with their own style that they really feel at home.

Situational Influences. The situation can also determine what might be considered appropriate behavior. Besides the formality or informality of the occasion, numerous other elements may govern conduct. These can include the content of the communication; the desired outcome; and recent, but perhaps unmentioned, events. Additionally, in some countries the buyer automatically assumes a higher status. Thus a person's relationship to you, as well as to others in the room, may play an important role in what would be regarded as proper behavior at that specific time. It is important, therefore, to take into consideration the various influences that may be coming into play when you observe conduct that seems out of character for that culture.

Study the Waters in Which You Travel

Interacting with people from another culture is like navigating unfamiliar waters laden with icebergs. Failing to acknowledge the below-surface portions is likely to result in collisions. The best strategy is to study the area and its characteristics as thoroughly as possible.

Geography. Knowing the geographical lay of the land means knowing the country's mountain ranges, waterways, natural resources, population density and distribution, states or prefectures, and major cities. Check out its coordinates: What are the neighboring countries or oceans? Terrain and demographics may affect distribution, and climate may affect transportation and storage. Highly dense cities may also create transportation problems. The total population will reflect the size of your prospective market, but the demographics will affect the feasibility. Densely populated countries, such as Singapore with 11,000 people per square mile or Taiwan with 1,450 people per square mile, will have radically different views of travel and space than the United States with 68

people per square mile or Canada with just 7. It's also important to
be aware of recurrent natural disasters or dangers. Hughes Space
and Communications Company learned an expensive lesson in
French Guiana, where a number of employees were stationed for a
satellite launch project. Although the company had made certain
jungle areas off limits to the employees, one decided to brave a
restricted area to fish for piranha and lost his finger in the process.

History. Knowing the history of a country means, at the very
minimum, the cultural history and major events that shaped its
value system. It means knowing its heroes and heroines, which will
give you an idea of its role models, as well as good topics for
conversation. It also means knowing its history with its neighboring countries. Many times the biggest conflicts are with those next
door. Knowing the history of the two countries may cause you to
think twice before saying to someone in Vietnam, "I just met with
a Cambodian; maybe we could do a three-way joint venture." Also,
knowing the history of Vietnam, you would be advised to sojourn
at the old DMZ with caution. Live mortars and mines still plague
the area.

Religion. Next, learn about their religion or religions. What are
their places and methods of worship? In many Buddhist cultures,
most of the religious observances are carried on by priests and
monks; for the average person, Buddhism is more a way of life than
weekly visits to a temple. On the other hand, Muslims must pray
five times a day, so many shops in these countries will close briefly
for this. If you are hosting an Islamic delegation, you may want to
take this custom into consideration. If you are traveling to a country, it will be essential to learn the religious holidays. Israel observes the Sabbath on Saturday and consequently closes stores on
Friday afternoon and Saturday. Many Islamic countries take Thurs-
day afternoon and Friday off and fast during the day for the month
of Ramadan, which is reckoned each year in accordance with the
lunar calendar.

The religion may greatly influence the attitude toward work.

Success may be considered to depend more on the will of God than on hard work or good strategy. Religions are often a key source of a culture's values. Remember that most people take their faith very seriously and are offended by critical questions or debate about their religion. It is not advisable, in many countries, to talk about the desirability of the separation of church and state or whether God exists. Also consider other religion-related traditions. Many Japanese would not want to work in a factory that had not been blessed by a Shinto priest. Other Asians may insist on consulting geomancers to determine the best places for things or the most auspicious days for important events.

Education. Take note of the major educational institutions in a country and their significance. Virtually every country has its cultural equivalent of Harvard and M.I.T., and businesspeople who have attended such high-profile schools gain instant status and inclusion in the business community. In an extreme example, the Eighth Class of the Korean Military was responsible for planning and carrying out the country's 1961 coup d'etat; ever since, members of this class from a prominent school are invested with social clout and recognized power.

In the legal field, most developing and newly industrialized countries honor law degrees from prominent schools in other countries more than those from indigenous schools, with one interesting exception. Singaporeans take great and deserved pride in the fact that most of the country's lawyers have degrees from the Law School of the National University of Singapore. "It's the only country in Asia that I know of where a local education in law is viewed as first-rate," says Hawaii-based international lawyer David Day, who has worked throughout Asia. It's important that you know this when engaging with lawyers in Singapore or elsewhere in Southeast Asia. In Malaysia, for instance, many lawyers have attended Singapore's law school or one in England; after they have earned a degree overseas, they will make note of the fact on their business card.

Deep Culture. Research values and priorities, belief systems, cultural assumptions, and superstitions. What types of goals do people hold? What are their views about quality of life? What things do people respect? What do they ridicule? Muslims, for example, respect religious people, but have no regard for atheists.

This sort of information will require a much deeper investigation than what you will find in most travel books. However, this knowledge will be indispensable for penetrating the "real" world that people of a country function in, and to avoid remaining a cultural outsider. Find out about their attitudes toward Americans: Are there deep resentments due to historical events? Are there emotion-laden value differences? Other Americans who have spent time there are a good source for this information.

Popular Culture. Find out about the most popular sports, games, and cinema. What are their native sports? Who are their athletic idols? During the 1994 soccer World Cup Competition, Antoine Morrison informed a client in the United States about how consumed with the sport people in Mexico (and much of the world) are, and how they consider people who are unaware of what is going on with the national team, known as the national selection, as virtual outsiders. He advised the client to learn the names and positions of the national selection, as well as the coach (called the Technical Director, or DT), and to follow the Cup matches closely. A week later the client phoned him with this message: "You know the deal we've been going nowhere on? When I phoned my Mexican counterpart the other day, I got the usual sense of indifference. Then I brought up the national selection and asked him if he thought the DT would play Hugo Sanchez or Carlos Hermosillo. I asked him to explain Mejia Baron's strategy. I couldn't believe it! His attitude changed immediately as we discussed Jorge Campos, Luis Garcia, and Zague. The destiny of the deal we were working on took a 180-degree turn!"

Subcultures and Regional Differences. Ethnic and religious groups can make up strong and sometimes economically important subcultures of a society; you need to become aware of how to cross these cultures while doing business in a single country. For example, Malaysia's business community consists of three distinct cultural groups: Malay (*bumiputera*), Chinese, and Indian (there is also a small Arab influence). When dealing with government officials, you can expect to be dealing with a Malay, who will likely be a Muslim; should you be involved with the Malaysian legal system, you may deal with more Indians; and if you need to speak to the managing director of a company, you will probably be dealing with an ethnic Chinese. In Hong Kong, you will perhaps deal with British, Indian, or American people, as well as with people of two conflicting Chinese cultural influences: mainland Chinese and Cantonese Chinese. Mainlanders carry all the baggage of their socialist history and speak Mandarin, while Cantonese Chinese, who were raised under British tutelage, may be wary of mainland Chinese and may feel superior to them in commercial know-how.

As far as the Arab world, says Dr. Kamal Naffa, a consultant from Jordan, "Arabs are not a homogenous people. There are tremendous variations and degrees in their social, cultural, and political development, extending all the way from the highly sophisticated to the primitive. Arabs in Lebanon, Jordan, Syria, and Egypt behave and think differently from Arabs in the Gulf states. Their values, attitudes, and orientations are quite different. In Jordan and Lebanon they eat with silverware, but in the Gulf they enjoy sitting on the floor and eating with their hands in the traditional manner. In the northern states wives are expected to join their husbands in welcoming a guest and socializing with them, while in the southern states (Saudi Arabia and the Gulf states) social mixing is taboo."

What are the minority and immigrant groups, and what role do they play in the economy? In Vietnam, the 500,000 people of Chinese descent, who live primarily in the south of the country, may wield little power in the corridors of government, but they virtually control the large-scale wholesaling system for the entire country. If you want to distribute a product to Vietnam's newly emerged market of 70 million budding consumers, you will likely need to deal with both Vietnamese officials as well as Cantonese-speaking Chinese, known as the *Chaozhouese*. Further, try to ascertain the degree of assimilation of the minority group into the mainstream. Again in Vietnam, because of their harsh treatment at the hands of Vietnam's government during the 1970s and 1980s, Chinese businesspeople continue to be secretive about their commercial activities.

Cross-Cultural Training

To encourage cultural sensitivity throughout your firm, training is the solution. The impetus at a company for initiating cross-cultural training is normally a blow-up with a foreign partner over a culture-related issue, though more and more firms are conducting training with *prevention* of costly mistakes in mind.

Two things were instrumental in convincing Hughes Space and Communications Company executives to initiate cross-cultural business training conducted by outside trainers, says division administration manager Karen Rakita. First, in the mid-1980s Hughes had decided to diversify its space and telecommunications business to create a better balance between commercial and government contracts. In doing so, the company needed to "attempt to build better international business relationships," not only with foreign governments but with entrepreneurial private companies as well. Second, this attempt was not going smoothly. "Communications were difficult. The cultural differences in negotiating styles were exacerbating contract finalization, and some customers were perceiving our American style as arrogant." So in response, senior people at the company "got behind the idea that we didn't have all the answers, but maybe we could learn." Individual business units began running day-long cross-cultural seminars on the countries where they had customers, including Indonesia, China, Japan, Mexico, and Malaysia.

Ford Motor Company began training its people in a more preventive manner. The company does more business with Japanese firms than any U.S. company: it owns 25 percent of Mazda, builds a minivan in a joint venture with Nissan, and buys and sells a myriad of Japanese automobile components. "Proactive and direct is the approach Ford uses to develop competence in employees who interact with the Japanese," says Joe Gilmore, the Ford executive in charge of the firm's minivan project with Nissan. "This occurs through a variety of practices, including programs that help Ford personnel better understand Japanese culture and negotiating practices and by encouraging the study of the spoken language."[1]

Sometimes a globally minded executive knows something that upper management should know but can't get anyone to listen. When your boss or staff won't listen to you about what should be changed in your firm's international approach, it might be time to bring in the hired gun, someone with the knowledge and credentials to reinforce what you've been trying to tell them. Harbo Jensen tells us that the training initiative at Chevron began this way. Chevron's agreement in Japan—the largest joint venture in Japan between Nippon Oil and Caltex—is five pages long double-spaced and is in both English and Japanese. The agreement was signed just after the Second World War, and has been very successful. "The agreement says just that we're going to work together in the refining and marketing business. There was a lot of [dependency] on the handshake," says Jensen.

In the 1980s, Chevron people began coming to Jensen saying that they'd read Chevron's agreement with the Japanese, and had lawyers go over it, and that if Chevron wanted to, it could exploit opportunities in Japan outside the joint venture, such as, having an operating company move into another operating company's area. "I told them that in Japan that's not done," says Jensen. "There's nothing in there that says we can't go into Japan and take their customers away from them. But there's a different mindset between people who are used to looking at the details and working to craft an agreement very precisely, versus the old traditional approach." That's what led to Jensen bringing in Rowland & Associates to educate Chevron executives. "They didn't believe me," says Jensen with humor. "You never believe your own employees, but they will believe someone from outside."

Culture trainings help your staff develop awareness of cultural differences between themselves and others and determine how responses to these cultural differences can heighten commercial success. Use training to instill staff with a knowledge of the region they are dealing with: how to adapt to the local cultures, how to work with the employees, how to travel and live in the region, and how to speak a bit of the local language. In a day's training, a team of people can walk away with a beginning knowledge of the culture, customs, spoken languages, climate, geography, values, history, food, money, essential protocol, and communicating and bargaining style.

Prepare a Culture Manual

In lieu of hands-on training, a company should make its overseas employees aware of the cultures with which they are to deal. Create a library of books if you can, or at the very least develop a manual. A Texas oil company prepared such a manual before sending employees into a South American jungle populated by a native people. An excerpt from its employee manual is illustrative.

> You are a guest in Waotrani territory. They expect you to show absolute respect for their customs, their belongings, their families, and especially their women.
> All contacts with the Waotrani should be avoided. How-

ever, if you have an unforeseen encounter with a Wao, keep calm. Remember that, in general, the Waotrani are always armed with spears and shotguns for protection and hunting and that they speak loudly and make many gestures. You should not think that these are signs of attack. Do not show fear or make any gesture that might seem aggressive. Tell the Wao that you are his friend and, looking at his face, repeat these words: "Waponi, amigo Waotrani boto Maxus." ("Greetings, Waotrani friend, I am Maxus.") Report to your supervisor so that he can talk to the Wao and resolve the situation.

The Waotrani believe in common ownership. For them everything belongs to everyone. Their concept of private property is not the same as ours. If you understand this idea then you will also understand why they come into camps and working areas and ask for things. We are in their territory, and they consider our belongings to be for common use. Do not keep food in the open. To find food and not to take it is unthinkable for the Waotrani. If there are any requests for tools, objects, or food, contact Maxus Community Relations immediately. If the demand is urgent offer the Waotrani some food.

The Waotrani's past is full of violence: tribal wars, fights with trespassers, and fights for personal revenge. Although nowadays the Waotrani are better aligned with Western customs, they still firmly believe that an offense must be avenged and that, like good hunters, they must defend their women, territory, animals, and farms.

Like all human beings, the Waotrani are jealous about women. Any insinuation could be interpreted as flirting. You must treat Waotrani women the same way you would like strangers to treat your own wife and daughters.

You offend a Wao if you make a promise that you do not

keep. Never offer something that you cannot give, and never lie just to get rid of a problem. Say simply "No" or "Wait, let me ask if I can do this."

If you offend a Wao, he will never argue back; he will merely go away quietly. However, he might return without your knowledge for the purpose of killing. A Wao never threatens; he takes direct action.

You must respect the Waotrani culture. Do not offend the Waotrani and do not lie to them. Your life and your work depend on it. We and they are equals; our differences are in our respective cultures and histories.[2]

Do You Adapt Well to Cultural Difference?

To find out, you can formally test yourself for cross-cultural adaptability. Perhaps the finest cultural adaptability test—the Cross-Cultural Adaptability Inventory (CCAI)—was developed by Dr. Colleen Kelley and Dr. Judith Meyers. "We developed the inventory as a training instrument," says Kelley, "[for people] to assess themselves in order to work at their areas of strength and weakness. Some people look at the results and decide that [an international position] is not for them and they drop out, while others address their weaknesses."

The four "dimensions" of the CCAI are based on an extensive search of the cross-cultural literature, test surveys, and exhaustive research. The four dimensions reflect areas of "aptitude" desirable in those who must deal with cross-cultural challenges like working with a foreign partner or living overseas. You may want to take the test yourself to improve your weaker "dimensions" or have your staff do so to help them improve. The desired capabilities are listed below.

Emotional Resilience. The people with this trait can be said to have equilibrium of feelings. When they are thrown off balance, they have the ability to recenter and regroup quickly. The attribute is associated with a generally positive attitude and a healthy sense of adventure. These characteristics are important when a person deals with the unknowns of an unfamiliar culture, which can result in frustration, a sense of failure, disappointment, and sudden depression.

Flexibility/Openness. This is a more mental—rather than emotional—dimension that has to do with the liking of new ideas. These people are simply open to new ideas and stimuli; they have an affinity for differences, including different types of people—obviously a desirable attribute for anyone going to another country where differences are part of the territory.

Perceptual Acuity. This one refers to an ability to focus on verbal, nonverbal, and contextual clues in conversation and to accurately interpret them. These people are otherwise known as "sensitive" to their surroundings, an important competency for anyone participating in a cultural interaction where messages are veiled or not explicitly expressed.

Personal Autonomy. These individuals possess a deep-seated sense of their own identity apart from the culture, such that when in another culture they don't lose a sense of identity. They have an internalized sense of values and identity that stays in place even when engulfed in another culture for an extended period of time. The attribute is associated with strong self-respect.

Part I: Assessing Yourself for Cultural Empathy

Answer each item by circling the appropriate number on the continuum below:

To Almost No Extent			To Some Extent		To a Great Extent			To a Very Great Extent	
1	2	3	4	5	6	7	8	9	10

I make the effort to learn about the cultural background of a place before doing business there.

1   2   3   4   5   6   7   8   9   10

I get along well with people I work with no matter what their cultural background.

1   2   3   4   5   6   7   8   9   10

When I interact with businesspeople from other cultures, I do so aware that my behavior is influenced by my own cultural values and beliefs.

1   2   3   4   5   6   7   8   9   10

When I do not understand a behavior or trait among members of another culture, I find a way to politely ask them so that I can better understand and feel more comfortable.

1   2   3   4   5   6   7   8   9   10

I am at ease when overseas businesspeople ask me questions about my country, my culture, and my personal background.

1   2   3   4   5   6   7   8   9   10

Part II: Assessing Your Company for Cultural Empathy

My firm has come to realize that there is a "bottom-line" advantage to be gained by educating its international staff about the countries and cultures with which it does business.

1   2   3   4   5   6   7   8   9   10

My firm approaches other countries with an attitude that business cultures differ, and that the customer's cultural rules should be followed by the foreign company trying to do business there.

1   2   3   4   5   6   7   8   9   10

My company has clearly articulated its corporate values and priorities to its employees, who are expected to understand them.

1   2   3   4   5   6   7   8   9   10

My firm frowns on derogatory remarks made about members of other cultures, and actively attempts to dislodge stereotypes and images of people based on their national or ethnic group.

1   2   3   4   5   6   7   8   9   10

My company has sponsored "diversity training" to teach its employees to work together effectively despite their cultural differences.

1   2   3   4   5   6   7   8   9   10

If you or your firm scores 25 or lower out of a possible total of 50, the area of cultural awareness and empathy skill building should be a key priority for you and your company.

Acquiring Interpersonal Expertise

The first problem in cross-cultural communicating involves language. Throughout the world, 2,796 languages have been identified and easily three times as many dialects. Typical foreign language courses in America are French, German, or Spanish. Yet the top five spoken languages, ranked by the number of native speakers, are Chinese, English, Hindi, Russian, and Spanish. Few Americans are fluent in a second language, so it's a good thing that English has come to be the international business language. Still, learning another culture's language will give you an appreciation of cultural differences at a deep level. You gain acceptance into the culture; foreigners who speak the local language are treated more as insiders than those who don't.

The Language Problem

Even in the same language, words and expressions may have a very different meaning. Even in cultures as close to ours as those of central and northern Europe, we discover when flagging a bus in Hungary that the English word "bus" is similar to the word for *fornication* in Hungarian, and a phrase that sounds like "see ya" (szia) is used for *hello* and *good-bye* in Hungarian slang. As close as American and British English are, in America "one billion" means 1,000,000,000, but in England it means 1,000,000,000,000. An international company recently pitched the idea of selling foreign tours to hunting types wanting to shoot pheasant in Uzbekistan. The Russian marketing adviser at first thought the foreigner meant *peas-*

ants. The discussion followed this line until the distinction was made between a Uzbek pheasant and a Uzbek peasant.

Often words exist in one language without equivalents in another. What is left out in a language, however, may also be a telling reflection of a culture's view of life. Arabic has no exact word for "time," and Russian has no word for "fun." A culture may have many words to describe something prevalent or important. In the Eskimo Inuit language there are dozens of words for types of snow —crusty, slushy, powdery—but no generic word for simply "snow." In Japan, there are a multitude of words to describe types of personal relationships.

Most Widely Spoken Languages

1. Chinese (Mandarin)	1,093	million
2. English	450	million
3. Hindi	367	million
4. Spanish	352	million
5. Russian	204	million
6. Arabic	202	million
7. Bengali	187	million
8. Portuguese	175	million
9. Malay-Indonesian	145	million
10. Japanese	126	million
11. French	122	million

Note, however, that up to 600 million people worldwide speak English as a second or third language.

Source: Hammond Atlas of the World, 1994.

The Cultural Underpinnings of Communication Styles

Understanding the way people speak in their own language is critical to interpreting what they are trying to convey when they speak in yours. Without this knowledge we tend to assume a foreign person's words carry the same meaning as when spoken by a native speaker. The meanings of words, however, often differ. Even if everyone in the world spoke the same language, the words would have different meanings, reflecting cultural concepts, perspectives, and local usage. The definition of "friendly" might be "outgoing" in America, "respectfully polite" in Japan, and "generous" in the Middle East.

Communication goals in other cultures are often different from ours. Americans are very task oriented and communicate mostly to exchange information. In business language we want people to be clear, frank, and to get to the point quickly. In Thailand, people are more group oriented. The emphasis is on harmony, and business communication may revolve around establishing rapport, preserving harmony, cementing the business relationship, or just getting a "feel" for what the other is thinking. Arabs have a particularly ardent attachment to their language. Arabic is considered one of their greatest cultural treasures, their national language as well as their religious language. To many Arabs language is so important that speaking especially well is considered to be an artistic endeavor; they believe there is great value in talking just for the sake of talking. So you can see how what we think of as being considerate, like getting down to business quickly and not wasting the time of others, could appear rude, disrespectful, ignorant, and self-centered to others. It doesn't take much cultural ignorance to destroy trust—and a profitable relationship.

Implicit versus Explicit Style

When we speak to one another, we rely on the context of the communication, the situation or circumstances surrounding the communication, to convey much of the meaning. The more experience and information we share with another person, the more we can rely on the context and the less we need to be explicit in what we say. Thus, we can be less explicit with a close friend or family member than with a total stranger and still be just as well (or better) understood. Perhaps because Americans come from such diverse backgrounds, we have been encouraged to communicate explicitly and leave little to implication. We are therefore defined as an explicit society or culture. As members of an explicit society, we Americans try to include all relevant background information in our conversations and do not assume the listener necessarily understands the behind-the-scenes issues.

Some other cultures, however, rely more on context to communicate the most important information. Asians, Latin Americans, Arabs, and some Europeans have grown up assuming that critical information will often not be verbalized, but merely implied. These are considered implicit cultures. An American manager might speak directly and to the point to a subordinate: "I need the Delta project proposal as soon as possible." In an implicit culture, however, a manager might convey the same message by pausing by the subordinate's desk, asking him how he is doing, or by simply glancing at him in a meeting when the project is mentioned. The message is often indirect or merely inferred.

People in implicit societies try to extract background information on everything and continually look for meanings not readily apparent in conversation. Listeners are responsible for being able to extrapolate all the bits of necessary information from one statement. They can do this only by having a keen sense of observation and a tremendous amount of background information derived as much from informal networks and "informants" as from media or more formal information channels. They consider it critical to their relationship with you, and to the job at hand, that they have as much information as possible up front, before serious discussions begin.

It is not only how forthcoming people are in providing background information that distinguishes a society as explicit or implicit. For example, Americans tend to use words to achieve a resolution. Implicit societies, on the other hand, often use nonverbal methods to resolve a situation. In the American filibuster, congressmen try to obstruct legislation by making long speeches, and in the German *Papierkrieg,* or "paper war," one or both parties involved attempt delay by demanding endless paperwork from the other party. Japanese legislators, however, will exercise *gyūhosenjutsu,* or "the cow-walk strategy," taking 25 minutes to walk 20 yards to cast their vote—a nonverbal stalling tactic.

Explicit and implicit styles can easily clash in international communication or negotiation. To an American, someone who is being indirect or ambiguous is hiding something, and an American will often doubt that person's integrity, seeing him as cagey or deceptive. If the other person's manner of speaking is very roundabout, the American is likely to see this as wasting his time. Someone coming from an implicit society, however, is likely to find the direct American rude, coarse, and lacking in essential communication skills. Worse, unable to read between the lines, the American irritates the foreigner by articulating issues that were implied, and he persists in direct and open communication of delicate matters. Less able to read the surrounding signs, Americans are often seen as dense, or at least rather slow. We expect people to *tell* us all the pertinent information, and we often lack the background information and observation skills necessary to read between the lines. Americans become irritated when others seem magically to know when there is going to be a critical turn in events, because we are deficient in informal networks that act as "radar" and inform us of critical behind-the-scenes issues. People from implicit societies assume that others are gathering pertinent information from implication and context and they therefore tend to articulate less. As the American attempts to "get right to the point," he or she may miss many other critical points that could be garnered from a more circuitous process.

Problems can arise in the exchange of information as well. When we ask for information, we want it to be as correct, concise, and as conclusive as possible so we can make the best decision for ourselves, but people from implicit societies rarely "volunteer" information except to those with whom they have established some sort of reciprocal relationship. As good students of explicit values, we tend to be better speakers than listeners. We lack the skills to ask information-generating questions and the patience to wait for more, so we end up dominating the conversation. Consequently, not only do we come across as rude, but we often miss the opportunity to gather crucial pieces of information, ensuring that the exchange goes only one way—to them!

In order to communicate effectively in implicit societies, business partners must first establish a relationship. Where high reliance on context is essential, having a business discussion with a little-known party is virtually impossible. Without a personal relationship, the Arab, Asian, or Latino will consider it absurd to try to do business. Yet many Americans not only find establishing a personal relationship a waste of time, but also consider it irrelevant.

Let us emphasize here that neither style is bad or good, simply different. The key is to understand the difference and adjust your style accordingly.

The Linear versus the Polychronic Style

Much of the discomfort in international discourse between Western cultures and the rest of the world is due to different conceptions of time. The West operates in a world dominated by "linear time," where time is experienced sequentially—like a train moving down a track, with details organized in an orderly, "ducks in a row" manner. People are most concerned with the immediate future. When you ask Americans about their family, they will usually tell you about their children.

In contrast, most of the cultures of Asia, Africa, southern Europe, and Central and Latin America operate in polychronic (also called holistic or multidimensional) time, where communication flows in a more circular fashion. People are concerned not just with the immediate future but with the past and distant future as well. When you ask an Asian about his family, he will usually talk about his ancestors.

Linear people follow a sequential approach to solving problems, giving presentations, conducting negotiations, and accomplishing tasks. They much prefer a sequentially organized discussion to a circuitous one.

In the polychronic, or holistic, mode, however, time and events are seen as flowing simultaneously in many directions. Other events happening in these dimensions are equally pertinent to them, although their relevance to the immediate goals may be a mystery to you. Everything is seen as interrelated, and there is a more fluid approach to reaching goals, which are often considered to be the result of fulfilling relationships rather than completing a series of linear tasks. Consequently, polychronic people tend to be involved in many things at once and move easily between them, rather than finishing one before proceeding to the next.

It is important for them to have a historical perspective on events, so they are interested in learning the history of the other party. Although there is flexibility in superficial change, real change happens slowly. Even the very distant future, many generations away, is taken into consideration. It is helpful to understand that in the context of human history, most of the nonlinear cultures have been in existence far longer that ours and that these differences are deeply imbedded in each individual.

For the Western businessperson, operating in a polychronic culture may be distracting and unsettling. Success in a polychronic environment requires patience, flexibility, and a commitment to completing *human* transactions. Negotiations may be frequently interrupted, or a meeting agenda may be modified or even ignored while a circular or spiraling approach is employed to solve problems. It means also that your foreign counterpart may

- seem to talk in circles;
- expect you to be looking at other dimensions of a business relationship beyond the obvious tasks at hand;
- demand that you consider historical factors or the long-term implications of the proposal;
- jump around during meetings, with certain issues being rehashed numerous times from different perspectives, often communicating in a circular fashion.

The Public versus the Private Self

People around the world differ about how much they are willing to expose their private thoughts and personal life when communicating in public. Those who are accustomed to a great degree of self-disclosure often find those who customarily disclose less to be evasive, distant, and overly formal. Conversely, when those who characteristically expose less—and less frequently—are confronted with people who are comfortable with self-disclosure, they are often put off by the seeming lack of sensitivity, the physical and verbal assertiveness, and the disregard for formalities.

We Americans need to be sensitive and not destroy trust by

aggressively pushing our way into areas that other people feel are private. If we wish to probe further into the other person's private self, we will succeed more quickly by understanding our counterpart's need to establish a strong, trusting relationship before engaging in what he or she would consider more intimate discussions.

Confrontation versus Consensus

When relationships are considered the most critical element in business, the effort will be to create a consensus among the relevant parties rather than have one party be the winner and the other the loser. Americans tend to feel that open debate is the most efficient way to reach the best decision, but if others are alienated in the process, this approach can mean disaster.

The notion of the public forum as being appropriate for discussion of sensitive topics is anathema in most cultures that prize the preservation of face. We must remember that a challenge to another person's opinion may be seen as a personal attack. If you succeed in embarrassing one or more parties by "exposing" their weakness, it is likely they will find a way to undermine your proposal, even if others have decided it is best.

A Japanese participant in discussions, for example, may become taciturn after an American openly suggests that the problem is with the Japanese company. What is at stake is the person's "face," or sense of dignity. This is an important issue in all cultures, but some are much more sensitive to it than others. By approaching the disagreements in an indirect or implicit way, you can achieve a resolution while preserving everyone's face. While North Americans and northern Europeans may see direct confrontation as the most efficient and honest approach, most of the rest of the world find this insulting. The much-prized "art of persuasion" in America is seen in many other cultures as little more than antagonistic bullying.

Learn to consider the other's position or proposal before commenting; deliberating conscientiously shows you didn't disregard their opinion out of hand. Finding merit before suggesting potential problems can go a long way toward reducing resistance. Try to give credit to others; people know when it really belongs to you and will respect your humility. But even more important, when you refrain from "defeating" others, you acquire allies rather than enemies. When dealing with issues that are truly sensitive, find a way to talk around them indirectly. This will facilitate maintaining relationships as well as respect when working in implicit cultures, and you will be less apt to embarrass or alienate someone. It will also ultimately permit you to exert much more influence than if you were using a more aggressive, direct approach.

Style and Pacing

Different cultures have different linguistic styles. Americans tend toward a straightforward, direct form that makes the point early on. Many other cultures prefer a more colorful, poetic style that uses metaphor and hyperbole to add to the artistry. Arabs, in particular, prize eloquence and flowery, figurative language over mere content. To Americans, this style is, of course, inefficient and artificial. The adjectives are seen as overkill and the metaphors are sometimes taken literally. Yet for the Arabs, the American style seems unfeeling, two-dimensional, and lacking. Americans appear to lack skill in the art of locution. Developing the skill of eloquence, especially to the flowery degree used by Arabs, is difficult for most Americans, who have been taught from youth to "get to the point." Those who are successful, however, find the effort has usually paid off significantly in monetary results because of the sense of empathy it evokes and consequently the strong relationships they build.

Another difference in communication style is the pace, not only in speaking, but also in the timing of alternating between speakers. Brazilians frequently have two people talking at once in a conversation, with almost no pauses. Americans sometimes have brief pauses between speakers and sometimes have a little overlay of speakers. Japanese frequently have major pauses between speakers. If you are speaking with people from a culture that has many verbal overlays, such as the Brazilians, you may have to be more assertive if you want to participate in the conversation. Speaking when someone else is already talking may take some getting used to, but it will not be considered interrupting the way it would be in America.

If you are speaking with people from a culture with more verbal pauses, you may have to learn to pause more often to make sure others get a chance to speak. When talking with a Japanese, it is typical for Americans to wait just long enough to become uncomfortable and then begin speaking again. The Japanese person, however, has remained silent to show respect for the speaker or the comment, and by the time he feels it is appropriate to say something, the American is already speaking again. The result is that we end up monopolizing conversations. In order to allow and encourage others to speak, cultivate a speaking manner that incorporates protracted and frequent pauses.

Humor as Defined by Culture

The use of humor graphically reveals how strongly communication is embedded in a culture. Every culture has a different style of humor and it is difficult, if not impossible, to translate jokes, so they are better left out of cross-cultural exchanges. Take the case of an American expatriate who began his speech with a joke he had specially prepared for the occasion. When the interpreter finished, everyone in the audience laughed, and he was pleased that his efforts had paid off so well. Later, however, a bilingual friend in the audience confessed that the translator had actually said, "This kind American has just told a joke that is very culturally bound. It makes no sense to us . . . so if you would all please laugh NOW!"

Another American at a dinner party among Mexican guests,

when asked about ethnic prejudice in the United States, answered by telling a joke about an ethnocentric Texan on an airliner that has lost its engines. The captain asks three passengers to volunteer to jump out of the plane so that it can glide to safety. A Frenchman gets up and shouts, "Vive la France," and jumps. Next, an Englishman yells, "God save the Queen," and jumps. Finally, the Texan gets up and says, "Remember the Alamo," and throws a Mexican out of the plane. Although the teller meant the joke to be on the American, his hosts took offense because they felt that it belittled Mexicans.

Some Americans use sarcasm as humor or as a response to frustrations. It's so second nature that many don't even realize they use it. While funny and appreciated here, sarcasm is uncommon in many areas of the world and can have an extremely negative effect. When you receive some unfortunate news, if you reply sarcastically, "Oh, that's just great!," your foreign counterpart may believe you. Thinking the news is great he may do his best to please you by producing more of its kind. To us, engaging in witty repartee is a sign of intelligence and quick wit; it's friendly and fun. Look out: this is not a universal style and runs the risk of being interpreted as a challenge. It may gain you points in New York but black marks in Beijing.

Specific Communication Skills

Build rapport to increase comfort and cooperation. In America, people often try to develop a rapport with coworkers and counterparts because it makes the work more enjoyable and makes it proceed more smoothly. In many cultures, however, building rapport with the people you do business with may be a prerequisite for doing business. It is thought you cannot trust people with whom you cannot build rapport. And since most countries are less legalistic than the United States, trust is one of the most critical elements of any business interaction. This goes beyond simply trusting the other party not to take advantage of you; it means being able to trust the other party to actively keep your interest in mind. In this sense, business relationships in many other countries are approached much more like partnerships.

Pay attention to verbal styles. People are primarily *visual, auditory,* or *kinesthetic* in their internal processing of outside stimuli. If you give people information in the way they can process it best, they will be able to relate to what you are saying more easily and more accurately. Fortunately, people normally offer clues to their preference by what they say. For example, *visual* people are usually fast talkers. They frequently use visual terms such as "it looks like," "apparently," "we see eye to eye," and "I see what you mean." These people will tend to understand information best if you paint a picture for them, figuratively in what you say, or by literally drawing a picture or diagram. Actually *show* them as much as you can. Come prepared with handsome charts, graphs, reports and documents. They react well to words like "picture," "focus," "perspective," and "vision."

Auditory people are good listeners. They often use expressions such as "that sounds good to me," "I hear you on that" and "it sounds like." These people will respond well to dialogue, words being their primary instrument for understanding. Make sure that what you are presenting is well organized. Take time to explain things to them verbally and to hear what they have to say. Try to schedule extra time just for conversing.

Finally, *kinesthetic* people are slow talkers concerned with feelings, both physical and emotional. They will use terms such as "I get the sense that," "we can handle that," and "I have a good feeling about this." Be prepared to "walk them through" your presentation. They will understand most readily if you let them experience it in some sort of hands-on way. They will respond best to words like "motivate," "pressure," "sensitive," and "inspiration."

It follows that if you are giving a presentation to a number of people, it greatly behooves you to make it visual and experiential as well as verbal. Remember that *everyone* uses all methods, but we tend to rely more heavily on one than the others.

Make your communication effective. What are your main points? What is the best sequence for introducing your ideas? Decide on a strategy for presenting your case in the most effective way possible.

Make the topic clear. Always announce a change in subject by saying something like, "Could we talk about tomorrow's plans now?" If you fail to do this, the overworked listener is often trying to understand what you are saying in the context of the last topic.

Try to have written support. Many people read English better than they speak it and can use the written document to verify their understanding of unclear points. This is especially important when using numbers, such as in pricing or specifications.

Slow down your tempo. Unless the person is virtually fluent in English, it will probably be necessary for him or her to be doing some sort of mental translating. This takes time, especially when trying to understand certain words in the context in which they are used. Try speaking no faster than the other person is speaking. This is harder than it sounds, but it will give you the added advantage of having time to choose the most appropriate and most unambiguous words (if that is your intention).

Speak clearly. Slowing down will also allow you to articulate your words fully. Try to use short, concise sentences. Emphasize key words.

Simplify your vocabulary. Try to use words within the range of the other person's English vocabulary. Try to choose words with a single meaning rather than ones that have multiple interpretations. "Accurate" has one meaning, whereas "right" has many. Avoid words with alternate meanings that are used more commonly. "Address" is used more often to mean a location than to mean "speak to a group or person." It is not necessary to speak only about simple concepts, but you should use words the other is more likely to understand.

Rephrase important points. You cannot assume *anything* is understood correctly the first time. Use different words to say the same thing or approach it from another angle, says Bill Pomeranz, senior vice president of Hughes Space and Communications Company. "You have to be able to sense the honest-to-God English skills of the people you're talking to. With people who don't speak English that well, you have to slow down, use small words, and repeat—especially if you're in a place where they can't tell you that they don't understand because culturally that's not done. You need to learn to pick up the clues indicating that they may not understand what they just agreed to."

Ask one question at a time. We often ask double questions such as "Do you want to stop and eat dinner now or work until we've finished?" This actually contains two questions. It is common for nonnative speakers to retain only the second question and answer that one. Give your listener a chance to answer one question before asking the next. Alternatively, you could give options: "We can do A, B, or C. Which would you like to do?"

Use open-ended questions when you can. Open-ended questions open the conversation up for more information. They begin with *what, who, how, when,* and *where,* and therefore require an answer that would supply more information than a simple yes or no. It is also one of the few methods for determining whether the listener understands. "Yes" is so easy to answer, it is an unreliable way to determine comprehension. Asking "why" can put a person on the defensive, however, so use it with caution.

Summarize what you have said whenever you can. If a listener has gotten lost in the explanation, this will still confirm what the main issues were.

Give the speaker encouragement and moral support. Nodding your head as another person is talking, and making small, positive interjections such as "I see" and "Go on," helps a nonnative speaker of English feel more confident.

Check your understanding. You can do this by using a technique called *active listening.* Summarize back to the other person your understanding of what you heard. This should simply be a restatement in your own words of what the person said, and should not contain any judgment or advice. It could be particularly critical to use this technique when speaking on the phone or when trying to understand crucial information. It may be useful to agree ahead of time to employ this as a checking device.

Pay particular attention to people's names. Make sure you are pronouncing these, as well as the name of their company, correctly. It is, of course, best to find this out ahead of time, but people usually prefer that you ask them for the proper pronunciation of their name rather than listen to you ravage it.

Don't take yes for an answer. If you are in one of the areas of the world where people hate to disappoint others by saying no, even if they mean it, investigate any affirmative answer that sounds at all dubious. Also remember that in many places a nodding head is simply a nodding head—not an indication of agreement.

Watch for feedback. Pay attention to whether your audience is becoming bored or distracted. Maybe they can't follow what you're saying. Be aware of irritation or annoyance. Maybe your behavior is perceived as arrogant. Watch for signs of discomfort. Maybe you're asking for something that puts the person in an awkward position.

In addition to paying attention, try to get feedback by gathering information. The trick is to elicit the information in a culturally productive way. Watch people around you to see what works there. Pick successful people and study their style. Be aware, though, that the method for gathering information may differ drastically, depending on whether you are trying to obtain the information from a superior or an inferior, a client or a vendor, a friend/colleague or a stranger.

It can also be extremely useful, if not essential in some cases, to have a "cultural informant," that is, someone who can explain the culture to you and interpret what you hear and observe for you. Even more important, this person can also give you feedback on your own behavior and what the interpretation of it is likely to be in that culture. Always try to get a second opinion on everything.

When you have a written document translated, look it over for obvious mistakes: Are proper names spelled correctly? Are the dates precise? If measurements have been changed to metric, are the conversions accurate? Make sure the document looks as professional as you would like. If you have any question about the quality of the document's translation, have it back-translated into English by another party. This is an added expense, but is the best means you have to check the caliber of the document your foreign counterparts will receive.

Essential Advice on Using Interpreters

Although many people around the world speak English as a second language, the degree of their fluency varies drastically. This makes it extremely difficult to determine if you are understood or if you, in turn, understand the nonnative speaker of English. Many people feel embarrassed to tell you they have not understood. In other situations the listener mistakenly believes he or she *has* understood and therefore will not strive to clarify the message.

Misunderstandings, of course, are not uncommon even between two native speakers of the same language. The possibilities for miscommunication, however, increase exponentially when the communicators are from different linguistic and cultural backgrounds, so you may wish to increase your odds for accuracy by employing the services of a skilled interpreter.

In most such situations we recommend that you hire your own interpreter, rather than relying on the foreign party. First, if it is up to them, they may feel they have someone in-house who can do the job, even if there is no objective means to determine that person's qualifications. The person may have spent some time abroad or have studied English for some years, but may be lacking the degree of fluency necessary to be an interpreter. Second, if you hire your own interpreter, and can use the same person repeatedly, he or she will become accustomed to your style and be more willing to give you frank feedback or advice on communicating with people from that culture. And third, if you are negotiating, you are at a severe disadvantage if you are expecting someone on the other side to be your mouthpiece and ears.

If you decide to engage an interpreter, be sure you hire a reputable translator with in-depth knowledge of the dialect and business terminology that will be used in the discussions. Additionally, you should brief the person thoroughly about the nature of your immediate and past business before the talks begin.

A word of warning here. Know that your counterparts may not trust your interpreter; don't trust theirs, either. Have *your* interpreter interrupt the dialogue to retranslate what their negotiator has said the minute you or your interpreter sense the translation is faulty or if the tone has changed at all. An old ploy is making believe you don't comprehend a language so that you can overhear unguarded conversations. Don't discuss sensitive issues with your colleagues around your negotiating counterparts. Since most international businesspeople can understand some English and few Americans speak the counterpart language, the trick could be reversed very successfully. Have a debriefing afterward to learn of anything the interpreter may have overheard and his or her feelings regarding the tone and inferences of your counterparts.

While you are speaking to your counterparts, don't go on at length without pausing for translation. This will increase the accuracy of the translation and show more respect to the person waiting to hear the translation. Be sure that you are making eye contact with your counterpart—not your interpreter. Remember whom you are trying to establish the relationship with.

Do not interrupt your interpreter while she or he is speaking *or* listening. More than just sounding rude, this often leads to misunderstandings.

Be careful about translating names or slogans into other languages. Chinese has been the bane of our soft drink industry. When Coca-Cola tried to translate its name phonetically, it came out to mean "bite the wax tadpole." Pepsi translated its slogan, "Come alive with Pepsi," only to find it meant "Pepsi-Cola tastes so good that your ancestors will come back from the dead." Of course, others destroy our language as well. A sign in a Bangkok temple reads: "It is forbidden to enter a woman—even a foreigner if dressed as a man." And further north a sign for donkey rides asks: "Would you like to ride on your own ass?"

Communication Subverters

There are a number of things you should try to refrain from doing.

Don't resort to pidgin English. Speaking in distorted or incorrect English not only reinforces confusing language, it can easily be interpreted as patronizing.

Don't keep asking, "Do you understand?" Besides being terribly annoying, it rarely produces anything worthwhile. Many people will simply choose to say yes rather than to look ignorant by repeatedly saying no.

Resist raising your voice. If the person is having a hard time understanding you, it is unlikely that increasing your volume will be effective. What is more common is that by appearing to be yelling at the person, you alienate that person and establish yourself in the eyes of all those within hearing range as being arrogant and ignorant.

Avoid using negative questions. Although in English we normally use the yes or no response to conform with the answer, in some languages these confirm whether the question is correct. A yes answer to the question, "Aren't you going?" may mean "Yes, you are right, I am not going," so a simple yes or no answer from you in response to a negative question may be misinterpreted.

Don't use slang, colloquialisms, or idiomatic expressions. Most people study a foreign language beginning with standard usage. Textbooks rarely teach slang, since it varies from location to location and can be very ephemeral. People often pick up American slang by watching American movies, but it is difficult to second-guess what a person will or will not have heard and understood. Even more difficult to eliminate from your speech, but just as perplexing, are idioms. These are words or expressions that have another, literal meaning that the foreigner is probably familiar with. If you say "that's a piece of cake," the person is likely to think he understands and assume you are indicating it is dessert time. Or he may think you are preparing to proceed to a sporting event when it's time to "get the ball rolling." You may be surprised how habitually and pervasively we use idioms.

Avoid information overload. This happens much more quickly when listening in a foreign language than in your own. It's as though some of your brain cells are used just for processing the foreign language. If you want to get a sense of how difficult it is for the other person, try studying a foreign language and relying on your language skill to conduct business for just one day. People who have experienced that challenge usually find it easier to use the above techniques and to be patient with those who are making the often-strenuous effort to speak in a second language. It's important to stay calm and not get frustrated. It's a challenge for both of you, but your display of patience will go a long way toward enhancing the relationship, not to mention increasing the communication.

Don't do all the talking. Besides losing information, you are likely to lose business. Don't interrupt and don't finish someone else's sentences. If you finish others' sentences in a way they hadn't intended, they may agree with you out of politeness. Inadvertently, you will have just contributed to miscommunication.

Getting Your Foreign Employees to Communicate

Many of the emerging countries are steeped in their authoritarian pasts. Constructive and equitable cross talk between managers and workers, or among workers themselves while managers are present, may simply not be happening. In Poland, Hungary, Vietnam, and all the other countries shedding the communist legacy, workers and managers remain very careful about how they speak about things, especially with foreigners and expecially about problems or conflicts related to their production unit. Many of the people you will work with will still not, for example, want to get into a meeting where they have to talk about problems.

Western managers of joint ventures in these societies have not put enough priority on talking with their local people about *how to communicate*. They talk a lot about contracts, the product line, delivery dates, and price. But an effort must also be made to legitimate the expression of concerns and opinions. It's easy to mistake the make-no-waves behavior of the local worker or manager as merely acquiescing, or being polite, without acknowledging the psychological dimension to be overcome. You need to explicitly give people *permission* to speak about their ideas for making improvements, for doing things better. And the channels for communicating these things must be openly articulated.

Provide your workers with basic information: How are their opinions to be acknowledged? Through which channels? Who will acknowledge them? How will their opinions be used? Is there some reward for expressing opinions? Clearly explain your philosophy about how problems should be discussed, how they get flagged, and how they should be brought to your attention. Explain to them how solutions will be arrived at through nonthreatening group discussion rather than by managerial fiat. Spend time on building trust and rapport with the people with whom you want to communicate freely. Repeatedly invite local workers and managers to feel safe in asking for help and let your actions show it is.

If your local counterpart and coworkers can feel perfectly at ease in coming to you with questions, suggestions, and even mistakes, you've got the communication battle won. On the other hand, if your people feel reluctant and uncomfortable revealing their opinions or weaknesses, you're in potentially big trouble.

Nonverbal Language

Communication can be intentional or unintentional, verbal or nonverbal, understood or misunderstood. What's more, it can be any combination of these. The verbal message, "We have to study your proposal further," may be understood, while the nonverbal message, "We're not interested," may be missed. Often our nonverbal communication is unintentional (a yawn) or even uncontrollable (a blush), yet these apsects communicate something to the person who observes them. Although often underestimated, the role of nonverbal messages in communication is crucial. In fact, the nonverbal aspect of communication is so important that when the verbal and nonverbal messages conflict, we usually believe the nonverbal: "He said he was glad to see me, but he sure didn't look like it!"

Nonverbal communication includes eye contact, gestures, facial expressions, silence, voice quality, colors, and symbols. It also includes proxemics (interpersonal distance), posture, physical contact, and dress. Anything on your part that another person hears, sees, feels, or smells, and then interprets in some way, becomes communication. We note carefully how people shake hands, whether they maintain eye contact, and whether they are "dressed for success."

The trouble is, the same nonverbal act may communicate something entirely different in another culture. The nonverbal indication of yes and no, for example, varies greatly. Mexicans and other Latin Americans often wave the index finger back and forth to say no. Bolivians and Ecuadorans may raise their hand, twisting it back and forth, to indicate no or no room (in the bus or taxi). In Greece, yes has traditionally been indicated by tilting the head from side to side. No is indicated by raising the chin and especially when accompanied by a "tch" sound of the tongue, it becomes clear to a persistent vendor that the item is not wanted (and it's sometimes the only way to get them to leave you alone). In Iran and Lebanon, a tilt of the head up means no and down means yes.

Since nonverbal messages don't often get translated, we tend to interpret them in our usual way or according to our own value system. Like verbal behavior, what is acceptable and appropriate nonverbal behavior is sometimes conveyed through specific instruction ("Look at me when I speak to you"). But most often, it's learned by watching others. We learn to attach meaning to what we see or do by how others respond to it. Thus, we interpret and act out the nonverbal side of communication automatically and unconsciously. An important study of nonverbal communication at Harvard University identified over 400,000 ways in which we communicate messages without speaking.

People from implicit societies tend to be much more adept at watching nonverbal cues because they play an even more important role in those cultures. Rather than relying on your words, they will be looking to your nonverbal messages for indications of sincerity, compatibility, and trustworthiness. This means you should identify and keep a check on your nonverbal communicators and, in addition, learn to become an astute observer of theirs. Many people won't openly communicate it would be to your advantage to delay further discussions, but will expect you to sense indications. Asians, in particular, are conditioned not to verbalize negations directly, and it's hard to counter someone's objections when you haven't even realized they have expressed them.

In a fascinating study, a Harvard professor tried to determine the root of a frequent complaint by African Americans that teachers and employers spoke down to them. He discovered that, in comparison to the obvious head nodding and "uh-huhs" of the Whites, the Black employees and students gave much more subtle nonverbal feedback to indicate they understood, and consequently the teacher or superior would often assume they had not understood and proceed to "overexplain" the issue. This has direct implications for managers. You have to be observant of less overt signs to indicate both "I need your help" and "enough already!"

John L. Graham, a professor at the Graduate School of Management at the University of California at Irvine, has been gathering a body of statistical data about cross-border negotiating and communication for the past 15 years. His systematic studies of the negotiation styles of more than 1,000 businesspeople from 15 countries (17 cultures) are authoritative and empirical proof that nonverbal communication patterns differ around the world; they can help us recognize our dissimilarities with foreign counterparts before we send unintended messages or misinterpret those of others.

The study itself was brilliantly conceived and administered. The 1,014 participants were all members of graduate-level executive education programs, with an average age of 35.6 years, and, most important for the study, all had over two years of business experience in their respective countries. Participants played roles as buyers and sellers in negotiation simulations, which were videotaped for later analysis. We have included a table below of the key statistical differences among nations in nonverbal behaviors.

Eye Contact. Looking at the table of Graham's results for "facial gazing," we find significant disparities in nonverbal patterns here too. Our habits and expectations regarding eye contact with others are so ingrained that when someone strays from our assumptions in this regard, it often triggers quite severe responses. If people stare too intensely, it feels invasive; if their gaze is not direct enough, they seem insecure or insincere. The trouble is that what is intense and what is not intense enough varies dramatically from culture to culture. In many Asian, African, Latin American, and Native American cultures, one should avoid direct eye contact with someone considered a superior (by age or status), since it could be interpreted as aggressive or disrespectful.

The intensity with which Arabs maintain eye contact often makes Americans squirm. Even between more similar cultures, the convention can vary dramatically. Sophisticated Brits tend not to look at the listener when they are speaking until they have finished. The listener, meanwhile, gazes at the speaker much more intently than is customary in the United States. People of equal status often have more eye contact in South America than in North America, whereas in many African countries there is little eye contact during conversations, even among equals.

Facial Expression. Facial expressions tell us much about a negotiator's mood, reactions, and intentions. Expressions may differ across cultures, however, and sometimes the Westerner is simply not able to "read" the facial expressions of a foreign counterpart. In fact, in his study Graham found that Americans tend to consider the Japanese negotiator "poker-faced" and difficult to read. However—and this is eye-opening—Graham counted the number of facial expressions used by American and Japanese test subjects, and the number was roughly the same! He concluded that Americans "wrongly describe Japanese as expressionless." They are simply unable to *read* many of those expressions.

The problem is that the meanings of facial expressions vary from culture to culture. Greeks may smile when they are angry or upset, as well as when they are happy. Asians frequently smile when they are embarrassed. Raising the eyebrows indicates money in Peru but agreement in Tonga. In America, widening the eyes usually denotes surprise, but the French may interpret this as a challenge, the Chinese as anger, and the Latin Americans as a request for help.

Silence *Is* Golden. Many cultures cultivate the ability to communicate without words. All Asians grow up learning to make a point through silence. Not only is the point made more effectively

Linguistic Aspects of Language and Nonverbal Behaviors

Bargaining Behaviors (per 30 minutes)

Nonverbal Behaviors

Cultures

	Japan	Korea	Taiwan	China*	Russia	Germany	U.K.	France	Spain	Brazil	Mexico	U.S.
Silent Periods The number of conversational gaps of 10 seconds or longer	2.5	0	0	2.3	3.7	0	2.5	1.0	0	0	1.1	1.7
Conversational Overlaps Number of interruptions	6.2	22.0	12.3	17.1	13.3	20.8	5.3	20.7	28.0	14.3	10.6	5.1
Facial Gazing Number of minutes negotiators spent looking at opponent's face	3.9	9.9	19.7	11.1	8.7	10.2	9.0	16.0	13.7	15.6	14.7	10.0
Touching Incidents of bargainers touching one another (not including handshaking)	0	0	0	0	0	0	0	0.1	0	4.7	0	0

* northern China (Tianjin and environs)

Source: A working paper by John L. Graham at the University of California, Irvine. Reprinted by permission of the author.

and more profoundly this way, it is thought to be a superior form of communication. As one Japanese remarked, "We aspire to have relationships where no words are necessary." They prefer to communicate through something called *haragei,* "belly art" or getting a "gut feeling." It's a way of gathering information by "getting the vibes" and using them to perceive the thoughts of their fellow team members or the opposing party. Koreans value being able to communicate through the eyes, called *nunchi,* or "reading the face." Not only Asians, but many other cultures, especially those in Africa and Scandinavia, value silent intervals. Far from being "dead air," they are considered a natural ebb in the flow of conversation. Sometimes silence shows respect for the person who has spoken or for the point that has been made. Whatever the reason, consider it a time to collect your thoughts, be intuitive, and develop strategy.

Silence is a serious communication issue because Americans become uncomfortable during such periods. The British, Japanese, and Russians are particularly fond of using silence as a way to express reluctance to agree or to criticize. Americans become anxious waiting out the pregnant pause, even though sales trainers attempt to teach us to use silence to our advantage.

Perhaps the most frequent strategic mistake that Americans make during negotiations is to try to fill in the silent periods. This does two things: it makes us do most of the talking (and when you're talking you're giving away information), and it tends to make us offer concessions when they are not necessary. If it comes to a point where you cannot tolerate it, it would be better to ask for a break than to start talking.

When negotiating, the key is to present your offer and wait out the ensuing silence. *Do not interrupt.* If you do, you indicate that you are weak in your resolve, flexible in your offer, and your proposal is flawed. Wait quietly and maintain your composure.

Mirror Nonverbal Behaviors to Increase Rapport

In psychological studies of cognitive behavior styles, it has been observed that when people are in a state of rapport, they tend to make similar movements at about the same time. In other words, when one scratches his head, so does the other. If one crosses her legs, the other person does as well. But what is more interesting is that if you artificially model the behavior of the other person, you can actively create a feeling of rapport between you. This is a technique called *mirroring*. When someone smiles and you smile back, you are naturally mirroring.

To make the mirroring technique work, it is important to move in a way that is natural. Be fluid in your actions and never mimic. In fact, it is better to delay your action slightly, and not make exactly the same gesture. If your counterpart leans forward and picks up her coffee cup, you might lean forward and touch yours. If he leans back and crosses his arms, you might just cross your arms. Sightly more subtle, but also significant in a state of rapport, are qualities of speech, such as rhythm, tone, volume, and speed. It can be extremely useful to be in sync with these also.

As well as helping you to build a rapport, mirroring the other party will help you to be appropriate in your cross-cultural behavior. It will keep you from speaking more quickly than the other person can understand; it will prevent you from speaking too loudly and from being too informal in your posture; it will help you to become aware of the many ways the other party might nonverbally be trying to communicate with you.

Advice for Women

Women often find it more difficult to do business in male-dominated societies. America, of course, is no exception, but it can be even more of a challenge for women to break into the business world in some other cultures. Although it is not uncommon for American women to have a more difficult time initially than men would, it is also not uncommon for many women to find that after they have cleared the preliminary hurdles, it is ultimately easier to work with these foreign men than with American men. What's more, the foreign men often end up preferring to work with American females over their American male colleagues. This is because, while appearing "macho" on the surface, these cultures often have communication values that more closely resemble those of American women than American men. Some of these are: the importance placed on relationships, sensitivity to loss of face, emphasis on non-verbal communication, use of intuition, interpersonal skills, and the proclivity to "read between the lines."

It will, however, be very important that foreign counterparts from male-oriented societies understand from the outset the positions and expertise of female team members. They may otherwise assume that the females constitute support staff, as would be the case in their countries. Send your team members' names, preceded by Ms. or Mr. and followed by their titles, in advance of the visit. Add a small biography of each, with their qualifications, experience, and responsibilities. In face-to-face introductions, it is often better to have a male team member make the introductions, verbally supplying some of the above information.

Many women find it beneficial to be less aggressive than they would in America. Few countries value aggressiveness as highly as this country. This is especially true when you are going against traditional roles. By focusing on developing the relationship and giving men who are not used to working with women the time to become comfortable with it, you will be building trust in the process. And in most cultures, success comes from building trusting relationships.

Keep in mind that we sometimes erroneously assume that America is the most progressive in terms of gender impartiality, and we frequently stereotype other cultures negatively in this regard.

While the United States has yet to elect a female president, numerous other male-dominated societies have had a female holding the chief public office, as, for example, Turkey, Pakistan, Canada, England, Israel, Bangladesh, Sri Lanka, and the Philippines. Even Japan has a female speaker of the house. Meanwhile, only about 1 percent of top management in U.S. corporations consists of women.

Part I: Assessing Your Interpersonal Communication Skills

Answer each item by circling the appropriate number on the continuum below:

To Almost No Extent		To Some Extent		To a Great Extent			To a Very Great Extent	
1	2	3	4	5	6	7	8	9	10

I enter a country realizing that the people there may not communicate in ways that I am accustomed to or feel comfortable with, *and* that I communicate in ways that they might not be accustomed to or feel comfortable with.

1   2   3   4   5   6   7   8   9   10

I learn a few greeting expressions in the language of the people I visit overseas.

1   2   3   4   5   6   7   8   9   10

I have my business card properly translated when traveling to a place where English is not the native language of commerce.

1   2   3   4   5   6   7   8   9   10

I adjust my behavior when engaging with foreign businesspeople, especially by trying to be more formal than usual.

1   2   3   4   5   6   7   8   9   10

I feel just as comfortable and confident communicating through an interpreter as with somebody in my native language.

1   2   3   4   5   6   7   8   9   10

Part II: Assessing Interpersonal Communication Skills at Your Company

My firm acknowledges that each culture has its own ways of communicating and that its overseas staff members must make adjustments in their communicating style to be effective.

1   2   3   4   5   6   7   8   9   10

My firm has a system in place for briefing its international staff on how to communicate in other countries *before* it sends people overseas.

1   2   3   4   5   6   7   8   9   10

When an interpreter is needed, my firm obtains one and provides the time for him/her to work with all staff who will be present at meetings, in order to rehearse key parts of the presentation.

1   2   3   4   5   6   7   8   9   10

My firm hires international staff, in part because they are fluent in languages spoken in important foreign markets.

1   2   3   4   5   6   7   8   9   10

My firm has conducted cultural sensitivity training of its staff on the countries it does business with, to help staff communicate better in other countries.

1   2   3   4   5   6   7   8   9   10

As before, add up your score for each section of this quiz. If you or your firm scores 25 or lower out of a possible total of 50, the area of interpersonal communication skills should be a key priority for you and your company.

Utilizing Global Negotiating Skills

Again and again, the American executive sets out to "go global" alone, underprepared, ill-informed on the negotiating norms of the target culture, and with a completely unrealistic assignment. Like a hero in a Hollywood western, these corporate sharpshooters aim to survive and prosper through instinct, determination, and American "know-how," or brute force if necessary. And like the fabled hero, they are under tremendous pressure to "bring back the goods." Yet, in an overwhelming majority of cases, they return empty-handed. It's been estimated, for example, that for every successful negotiation between American and Japanese firms, 24 end in failure.

The so-called John Wayne approach has failed American business because it ignores the cultural empathy and personal bonding vital for success in the international arena. It often sacrifices long-term strategy in favor of short-term gains. And it arms its advocates with a false sense of confidence.

Relationships First, Business Later

While heavy-handed pressure and persuasion may accelerate you toward your short-term objectives, the resentment they create will usually undermine your long-term success. This doesn't mean that some measure of control and influence is not desirable or possible, but it does mean that these are often best accomplished through connection and partnership rather than by convincing and persuading.

The principle of partnership is this: Success is achieved most easily and completely when both parties are fighting for a common goal rather than against each other. It often requires connecting or "bonding" with counterparts, exploring mutual interests, looking thoroughly for creative solutions, and seeking greater mutual benefit. Pursuing partnership is characterized by a focus on interests rather than issues, and anticipates the development of a long-term relationship between the players.

Americans often insist upon trying to transfer the American "style" of business negotiations into international settings, concentrating on the letter of the agreement and cutting past preliminary discussions to immediately address points of disagreement. The American negotiator, caught in the time crunch and motivated by a task orientation, is focused on the business at hand while dismissing the wider benefits of cooperation between the two sides of the negotiation. In virtually every other industrial country, however, business is consummated through the establishing of relationships. Mexican business consultant Antoine Morrison explains:

> Not long ago, a group of high-powered businessmen from New York arrived at their meeting in Mexico City, armed with minute-to-minute agendas, elaborate 120-page contracts, and detailed marketing plans. After handing out their material, they said they were pressed for time and would like to hurry up the meeting. The Mexicans were stunned and said little during the presentation. After the meeting, the Americans were satisfied they had made an excellent presentation and had succeeded. The Mexicans, on the other hand, were convinced that no further business was possible. Why the divergent conclusions? The Mexicans wanted to get to know their future business contacts over a long lunch. They felt humiliated that the meeting did not include a recognition that they were market experts in Mexico. It's best if all papers are kept in your briefcase

until the Mexican signals he is ready to proceed. This might be thirty minutes or three hours. He wants to get to know people first and documents later.

Throughout much of the world, the parties engaged in negotiation respond to, and indeed expect, negotiation tactics that go "beyond business." The need for connection is interwoven into all business transactions. A Middle Eastern carpet seller expects at least an hour's worth of protracted haggling from his customer before arriving at a satisfactory price. For him, time conducting business is not separate from the fabric of life, a tapestry woven of personal interaction. To deny him the hour is to deprive him of one of the ingredients that makes life rich. At the corporate level, a Japanese company and Taiwanese company invest two years and millions of dollars just "getting to know each other." Scores of people from each firm have spent countless evenings drinking *sake* and *shaohsing.* Says Mike Lorelli, president of Pizza Hut International,

> A part of what I do is negotiating, and I got to learn the differences, for instance, between negotiating with a northern European as opposed to a southern European. With the northern Europeans you can get away with yellow-page style, which means you can go right to the book and discuss your checklist of items, getting right to the hardcore negotiations. If you're dealing with a southern European, you want to do dinner with them—relationships come first —and you're probably better off not even bringing up the business during the first dinner; save it for the second meal.

Choosing a Time and Place

Have time on your side. Time is often the easiest way for one side to seize the advantage. If you have time constraints and your team is visiting a foreign country for negotiations, you may wish to conceal the length of time you expect to stay in the country. This prevents the other side from stalling to the last minute and extracting concessions. Secure an open-ended hotel reservation, or make a short reservation that is easily extended. As your deadline approaches, don't let it show through verbal or nonverbal clues. Always act as if you have at least as much time as the other side.

When visiting another country, your hosts may overwhelm you by filling every minute of your days with scheduled activities. Politely insist on time for relaxation, private debriefing, and brainstorming sessions. Your counterparts may be employing "tag teams" to fulfill various roles at different times.

Try to control the venue of the negotiation. The location of the negotiation session may grant an immediate advantage or disadvantage to your side. Much of our discussion has assumed an American negotiation team traveling abroad, but the obvious advantages of conducting negotiations in your "home court" should not be overlooked. Being in your own country, you have the advantage of quick access to all necessary information and human resources. In addition, a negotiation set in your own territory grants a sense of power to your team and eliminates the detriment of lost sleep due to travel.

In many cases, however, it will be necessary to travel to another country for negotiations, and by accepting, you grant psychological and physical advantages to your counterparts. It is for this reason that many international negotiations are set in neutral locations, in which neither country holds the upper hand. Even if this is not an option, you may still be able to take steps to arrange a neutral negotiating location within the host country. Reserving meeting space in your hotel, and assuring your counterparts that the arrangements "have already been made," may level the playing field. Another option is to have neutral space arranged by your go-between or another neutral party.

Gathering Information

It's been said that the definition of an American-Japanese joint venture is that the Japanese send 24 people over here to find out everything the Americans know, and the Americans send *one* person over there to *tell* them everything they know. Being an explicit society, Americans tend to be more skilled at talking than listening or asking questions. Consequently, information gathering is one of our weakest points—and yet gathering information effectively and extensively is an essential aspect of international success. Here's how to do it.

Prepare questions in advance. Know what you want to ask. People from implicit societies generally come to a meeting with well-prepared, often prewritten lists of questions and requests. It can be disconcerting when they start firing them off at the rate of one per nanosecond. If you are not equally prepared with your list, you may find yourself caught up in making sure you have adequate responses. It's easy to get overwhelmed and lose control of the meeting. As much as you might like to be spontaneous, nothing can take the place of preparation.

Know what your information objectives are. Know how you intend to procure the information. Research everything you can ahead of time and have a plan for getting the rest. Don't be afraid to ask for what you want, and prepare your questions in advance.

Build rapport. Having a good rapport with others makes them *want* to give you more information. People are naturally inclined to give more information to people they feel good about. (This is especially true for group-oriented societies that are hesitant to give information to outsiders.)

Let them *bring up business.* You can always get information on the other parties' priorities, without giving up anything yourself, by letting them bring up the business. Allow enough time for rapport to build.

Ask open-ended questions. As described in Strategy III, open-ended questions are so named because they open the conversation up for more information by precluding a simple yes or no answer. A restrictive question severely limits the information you can receive. And since many people commonly use "yes" to mean "I hear you," these kinds of questions rarely provide you with any real information. They may give you a narrow answer, so follow up with the question "What else do I need to know?"

Listen carefully and give supportive feedback. Listen carefully to your counterparts. Don't interrupt or finish sentences for them. Try to focus on what *they're* saying (or more important, what they're implying), not on what you're going to say next. Remember the explicitness of our society traps us into concentrating on how well we speak and often causes us to miss the subtleties of an implicit style of communication. Watch nonverbals and hesitancy of speech. Don't forget to give positive feedback, like saying, "I see," "Really," and "That's interesting." This small form of encouragement can go a long way to help the person you're talking to feel confident and comfortable. It can be discouraging for a person *not* to get this, especially when the person may already be feeling insecure about speaking in a foreign language. It draws the person out. Try to limit the amount you talk.

Check for misunderstandings. It's useful to start this with an apology: "I'm sorry I'm so slow to understand. Does this mean . . . ?" In technical communication without an interpreter, you may agree to summarize back to each other.

Establish and nourish "inside" friendships. Your counterparts may tend to take less initiative to do something that may put them personally on the line. They may be risk-averse and only willing to do things that seem safe. When asked individually, they may not feel comfortable imparting information, even if it's relatively public knowledge. They are probably afraid to take responsibility without consulting their superiors first.

Try to find someone who has more personal initiative or who has a stake in the project you are involved in. Take the time to develop a strong and trusting relationship. Help *him* to accomplish his goals as much as your own. Without it getting lopsided, go out of your way to provide him with bits of information that might interest him. Remember, though, that your counterpart must know that he can trust you to save his face. It is your obligation to protect your ally. Never let it be known to others that you have that information if it is in any way sensitive.

Use humility to get a frank opinion or more information. When asking for an opinion, if you make it obvious that you think your idea is terrific, you may not get a response that is much to the contrary. The last thing many people want to do is to embarrass you or cause you to feel rejected. You may get more honest feedback if you preface a question with, "This may not be the best way to do it, but what do you think of this idea?" Beginning your opinions with "perhaps" or "maybe" helps them to feel more comfortable offering theirs.

Mark things. Another way to help keep information flowing both ways is to itemize things as you give them out. For example, if they ask for ten things, rather than saying "Here are all the things you asked for," present them one by one. "Here is the blueprint you asked for and here is the spec sheet. And by the way, do you have the diagrams I asked for? Also, here is the price list; I'll try to get you the documentation tomorrow. Maybe at that time you'll have the answers to those other questions I asked."

If you have some relevant information you don't mind sharing, then do so, but let it *buy* you something. Even if the information is not important to you, don't act as though it's worthless. If you do, they certainly won't feel as if they owe you something valuable. Also, keep in mind that speaking slowly and pausing before you answer a question can make what you're imparting seem more important.

Use a team effort. By team effort or approach, we don't just mean your negotiating team, we mean your whole company. If you're having a hard time getting some information you need and don't really have an inside connection in the company, perhaps someone you know in a different division of your company does have a connection, or for whatever reason would be more able to procure the information. By all means try to elicit that person's help.

It is also extremely important to have a central point for collecting and disseminating information, such as a file containing all the latest issues and decisions. It could have updated, pertinent information about the company—for example, if it has just been listed on a stock exchange—and relevant information about their team members. It could contain information about gifts that have been exchanged, noting what was well received. It could include the names of everyone in your company who has had dealings with the firm, giving the dates and subject of interaction so that readers of the file would know where to go for more detailed information. This file could also reiterate sensitive information that is not to be discussed (or perhaps some relevant information that was inadvertently gathered from a trip).

This can also help you maintain consistency. Very often our marketing, manufacturing, and research and development departments are not in close contact with each other. This means that after negotiating with your marketing people, your foreign counterparts may talk directly with the manufacturing people and be alarmed if they get a different opinion or story.

Make sure everyone on your team knows what information you would like to acquire. If you are splitting up, assign different people to collect different information that you can put together later. Assign someone on your team to take notes on everything—even nonverbal responses. The importance of this cannot be overemphasized.

An incorrect statement can sometimes produce results. This technique should be used with care, but stating something that is not accurate may produce the correct information in cases where you're not getting results in any other way. You can say something like "I understand you intend to have the project completed [or come out with your new product] in October." Many people use this technique in the form of writing a "stupid" proposal to encourage information from the other side.

At the very least, make conclusive notes as soon as possible afterward while you debrief with your team. Try to put everything together while it is still fresh in your mind. If you are overseas, talk it out into a microcassette tape recorder.

Report proceedings to your company. Following the visit, write up what happened in detail so that others in your company can benefit. If you have been refused access to one of their labs or locations while you were there, for example, your company should know about it and complementary action should be taken. Try to keep things balanced.

Protecting Sensitive Information

If you have sensitive information that others would be interested in, you need to take steps to protect it. *They* may have a strategy to get it. For example, if you have a delegation traveling to their company, they may divide you up and ask each person a different question. They may use people outside their company if and when they can. If they know that you are meeting with a government official, for instance, they might ask him to ask you a seemingly innocuous question for a piece to the puzzle.

If one of their teams comes to the United States visiting your various offices or labs, they may ask different questions at different locations that make them seem innocent but that can actually be put together later to get a clear picture. A visiting delegation has been known to "borrow" a notebook from an American's desk here and fax the contents back home during the night.

Know in advance what you will and will not talk about. Assign who will talk about what. Don't talk about someone else's project; you may not realize how sensitive some of the details are. Make sure you know exactly what has been covered by contract and what your company would rather not divulge.

Stop to think before you answer questions. Many people don't expect the immediate responses that we do in America. They like to get clear in their minds what they will say before answering. This gives you time to weigh things before you reply, and it makes it appear as though the information you're imparting is important.

Don't count on confidentiality. Don't think that something you say "just between you and me" won't get back to their company. It could be a serious mistake to underestimate company loyalties. Don't let intimations on the part of your counterpart lull you into thinking that things you say will be held in strict confidence.

Ascertain their reason for asking the question. This can give you some important information about their priorities and can help you avoid answering more than you need to.

If you cannot answer, say it is "classified." Proprietary information need not be divulged, but by expressing regret that you cannot ("I'm very sorry, but I am not at liberty to discuss that topic"), the all-important good relationship will be preserved. You can also simply change the subject, not say anything and out-silence them, or answer with another question, such as "Is this something your company is currently interested in?"

Selecting an Effective Negotiating Team

With group-oriented societies, you will probably discover that more may be gained by being a team player than by trying to be an independent task achiever. This means, for example, avoiding an adversarial position. It also means that negotiating against a team as an individual may put you in a weak position, making it appear as if you are too unimportant to have a team working with you.

Team building begins with the selection of appropriate team members. Some team members should be selected for their technical knowledge, others for their international experience, and, as mentioned, you should consider including one or more members with no assigned role other than to observe and take notes. Effective team selection means recognizing various skills in potential team members and further developing or acquiring the required skills as individuals and as a group.

The next step in team preparation is defining a hierarchy and specialized roles within the team. Often American negotiating teams make it difficult for their counterparts to recognize the relative importance of various team members. It can be confusing, for example, if the engineer overrides the team leader's opinion or a team member responds to a question without first deferring to a superior. The team leader should define in writing each member's position on the team and should stress to his or her group the need to comply to this hierarchy in introductions, seating arrangements, and responding to questions.

Status and hierarchy contribute to the negotiating team's overall goal of presenting a *united front* to the other group. Team members should not openly disagree with each other during discussions, nor should junior members supersede their assigned status. This constraint also compels a team to devise a series of verbal and nonverbal signals in order to communicate effectively. These techniques should be simple and applicable to a variety of situations. A cough, a scratch on the head, a tap of the pen may all be imbedded with a secret meaning. American negotiators have even been known to successfully use pig Latin in international settings as a means for on-the-spot private discussions.

Team leaders should be proactive in developing these techniques among the team members. Prepare the team to control their nonverbal cues at all times, and to give presenters on both sides of the table positive, nonverbal feedback. A team's communication strategies should also be realistic. Recently a company set out to engage in a series of negotiations with a potential foreign partner for the licensing of an advanced high-technology production process. The company's team felt they required a nonverbal signal to indicate when a member was releasing sensitive or privileged information too soon and should quit talking. It was agreed that in such a situation a team member would spill his coffee. After four days marked by several "mishaps," a member of the foreign team was heard to remark that he had never seen such a clumsy group of Americans.

Rehearse your negotiating team. Prior to the beginning of negotiations, the team leader should make sure the team members are aware of all the negotiating issues discussed earlier in this chapter. Make sure that the members of your team have a working awareness of critical aspects of the major religions in the country and the essential protocol. Work with your team to review basic phrases in the language of the country, and apprise them of the sensitive cultural topics not to be discussed.

Review the likely meeting format for the negotiation. Ascertain the traditional manner of greeting and seating arrangements. Decide who on your team will be responsible for introducing your delegation at the beginning of the session. Will the introductions be formal? In what order will your delegation be introduced? Will someone be expected to give a formal introduction of the company? Have the answers to these questions *before* stepping onto foreign soil.

Every member of your team must be apprised of the parameters for discussion. It can be especially effective to assign members of your team to handle questions on selected topics.

Decide who on your team will be responsible for giving an initial presentation introducing your company, its products, and the broad objectives of the negotiations. Have that member rehearse this material in front of your entire team to ensure that everyone is "on board" about the content of the introduction. If your company has had an interaction with the other company in the past, you should be prepared to include references to those as well.

Every member of the team should be able to answer a number questions, including:

- What is the history of your company?
- What is the background of your company's key executives?
- What has been the evolution of your company's activities internationally?
- How many employees work for your company?
- Who are your domestic and international competitors?
- What are your company's current production levels?
- How does the quality of your company's products compare to your major competitors'?
- What are the domestic prices of your major products?

Successful international negotiations require that the negotiating team take a consistent approach to the negotiation process. In addition, the team must be backed by a clear and firm commitment from the home office to the international initiatives under consideration. Backstepping or vacillating levels of support from higher echelons within the organization can fatally undermine the credibility of a company's representatives abroad.

One telecommunications subsidiary experienced a terrible situation when its president was suddenly given his walking papers by the parent company while its team was conducting a megadeal negotiation in Japan. Before the American front-line negotiators were informed of the change, the ex-president called to offer his services to the Japanese company. The Japanese negotiators opened the day's discussions saying how shocked they were at his removal. The poor Americans were dumbfounded and subsequently weakened in the discussions because of their perceived lack of support from the home office.

Redirecting the Momentum of the Other Negotiator

Aikidō, literally the way of spiritual blending, is a martial art developed in this century by a Japanese master. It synthesizes much of the Asian approach to gaining influence over another and involves redirecting the momentum of the other party toward your end, rather than opposing it with force. Imagine a flash flood rushing toward a town. Attempting to block it and push it back up the way it came takes significantly more energy than redirecting it.

The *aikidō* approach advocates going with the flow to get where you want to go. If you wish to cross a stream with a very strong current, you could lose your battle if you fight the current. If, however, you cross it while letting the current carry you downstream, you will have the energy to control where you get out and to then walk back upstream if you so desire. In the words of *aikidō* founder Morihei Ueshiba, "The mistake is to begin to think that *budō* [the way of the warrior] means to have an opponent or enemy, somebody you want to be stronger than, someone you want to throw down. In true *budō* there is no enemy or opponent. True *budō* is to become one with the universe."

In negotiation, gaining this control of redirection first requires connecting with the other person. Connecting is more than contact. With contact you can still only effect a change by pushing or pulling. But connecting implies blending, or becoming one, with the opponent's spirit or will. Once a true connection is made, drawing the other party in the direction you desire requires little or no force. The Westerner tends to counter force with force, or use a tough-guy approach, trying to out-muscle or intimidate the other side. But more sophisticated techniques involve controlling the outcome by connecting and redirecting the force of your opponent. The following are some techniques of "redirection."

Use questions to guide the meeting. Questions can be artfully employed to guide the meeting in a particular direction. Use questions first to gather information—to fully understand the momentum and direction of another team's position. Questions elicit hidden information about the strength of your counterpart's position. A strong answer could imply you should compromise on the issue, while a weak response may reflect a weak position that should prompt a concession from their side. Once you have the information you need, use questions to draw your opponent in the direction you desire, rather than push your agenda or position. This is a particularly powerful way to maintain control. It puts you in the lead and the other party in the position of responding to you.

Offer emotional support. Most people want the other side to hear, understand, and sympathize with their position, even if they agree with the other side's offer. This is part of connecting. They feel it is important to consider everyone's point of view, to empathize and to show emotional support, with such comments as, "I understand the difficulty of your situation." Emotional support does not necessarily imply a concession on your part, but it may feel like it to them, encouraging them to offer you a concession.

Present positive points. Americans often concentrate on areas of disagreement and attempt to get them hammered out. With the precariousness of intercultural relationships, however, it's usually better to emphasize areas of agreement. If there is enough agreement, both parties are more motivated to work hard to iron out differences. If everything seems negative, given the difficulty of working in unfamiliar circumstances, people are more tempted to throw in the towel. In areas where you do not agree, you should point to the *external* problems that shape your circumstance, rather than focusing on internal difficulties. Clarify your situation. By explaining your circumstances clearly, you are inviting the other side to empathize with you.

Make use of informal channels. Informal channels can include individuals who do not have a formal role in the negotiation. Intermediaries can often exert influence that would seem too forceful if coming directly from you. Informal channels also means using an informal setting to have a different sort of communication with your counterparts than you have in the "formal" meetings. In most cultures, the setting determines how directly issues may be discussed. What can be communicated "off the record" may make all the difference.

Highlight joint benefits. The mutual-benefit approach is a powerful motivator. This draws the other side to work with, rather than against, you. But it requires showing how you're part of the solution, not the problem—how what you're presenting is the best for all concerned, not just yourself. Try always to move the focus from conflicting issues to a joint solution.

Pay attention to your counterpart's needs. Many negotiators greatly fear letting down their colleagues and losing face. Peer pressure and sense of responsibility to their company or division often make them feel they are caught in the middle. If you can help save someone's face, they will forever be indebted to you. On the other hand, if you cause someone to lose face, they will never forgive you. Whatever happens, no one should publicly be made to look foolish or responsible for an error. One of the most critical skills to learn is how to be agreeable without agreeing, and how to disagree without being disagreeable.

Conflict Doesn't Need to Mean Combat

When disagreements or conflicts arise, the goal should be to restore the harmony and maintain the connection. This is not achieved by simply giving in, nor is it achieved by losing your temper. To be in control of a situation, you must first be in control of yourself. If you have determined that the only productive response is to raise your voice (in a culture where that is customary), then choosing to do so is a reflection of strategy rather than lack of control.

During the process of negotiations, your teams may reach an impasse. Consider the following questions.

Does this really matter? For Westerners, the contract, agreement, or letter of intent has traditionally served as the focal point of the negotiation process. As such, disagreements about the content of these are considered a roadblock, a problem that must be "solved" before the negotiations can proceed. In contrast, many other cultures view the economic issues as the context of the negotiation, rather than its focal point. To them, the most important goal is the establishment of a harmonious relationship that will reap long-term benefits. The details of the agreement will work themselves out in due time. An effective international negotiating team should be ready to move around points of conflict for the moment, and continue to work on the formation of a positive, productive relationship. As a corollary to this point, teams should not anticipate granting or receiving concessions until all the issues have been revealed and examined.

What are the alternatives? Firms should consider early on the alternatives to the negotiation being successfully completed in the manner they intended. By designing what the Harvard Negotiation Project calls BATNA, or the *best alternative to a negotiated agreement*, the team can analyze other approaches to the situation and employ it as a negotiation tool. The BATNA should be used as a standard by which to measure the terms of the agreement. Instead of refusing to compromise on an imaginary "bottom line," negotiating teams should compare alternative proposals in search of a compromise that will satisfy the interests of both sides. Thus it may also be used to devise creative solutions when an impasse occurs.

Don't Split the Difference

In many negotiations, the parties eventually agree to various compromises and concessions that amount to "splitting the difference" in order to proceed with a deal. No one side can be said to have out-negotiated the other. American negotiators are especially good at this form of bargaining; they weigh each issue and, after haggling for a while, give and take until both sides share equally in the burdens and the rewards of a transaction.

Our traditional negotiation model has been a contest—a rivalry where one's personal gains were directly proportionate to the other party's losses. This is a zero-sum game, where there is only so much in the pot and the amount of gains and losses equal zero in the end. Based on those rules, the only scenario where no one loses is when both parties end up with equal amounts. In negotiations, this motivates us to "split the difference." If you want to sell something for $30 and I want to buy it for $20, we can split the difference between our prices and agree on $25. Within the win/lose paradigm this is considered the "fairest" approach.

If we choose not to see negotiations as a contest, however, we are free to create an entirely new set of rules and results. In the previous example, where I only have $20 to buy your $30 item, I may find I have an unwanted possession you would gladly take as compensation for the $10 lacking in my offer. The other problem with splitting the difference is that often—and this is especially true in international settings—the strategy is unworkable. Sometimes a deal cannot be forged without a creative solution.

John Barry, president of a negotiation training company, uses the following corporate anecdote to illustrate to his clients that sometimes orthodox transactions can't work, and that creatively conceived ones can turn them into deals that do work:

> Kodak was negotiating with a new supplier. Discussion focused on unit price, with each side seeking to "split the difference" and come to a fair compromise. The supplier was a small operation, however, and without economy of scale on their side, they could not lower the unit cost to a point even close to what Kodak expected. Both sides were aggravated to the point of calling off discussions. Fortunately, however, they pursued a creative solution, and opened discussions on how Kodak could help the supplier

upgrade its manufacturing operations and thus build its product at lower cost.

A joint manufacturing arrangement was the result whereby the supplier was able to achieve lower unit cost, and Kodak was able to buy a needed product from a one-of-a-kind supplier at an affordable price. The deal turned out to be more complex than the original one, but it was advantageous for both sides. Without such a creative solution, the two companies would have left the table and failed to reach any agreement at all.

In order for us to come up with these settlements, the parties must first discard the notion that the numbers on the table, like chips in a poker game, are all they have to work with. They must next share a great deal of information about what they want, what they need, what they have, what they like, and so on. In many cultures this is part of that extensive "getting to know the other party" stage, and it can seem like wasted time. In the end, however, it can develop not only trust but the groundwork for finding truly creative solutions.

Answer each item by circling the appropriate number on the continuum below:

To Almost No Extent		To Some Extent		To a Great Extent		To a Very Great Extent	
1	2	3	4	5	6	7	8	9	10

I enter every negotiation with a list of questions to ask the other side in order to keep the discussion going, gather as much information as possible, and guide the discussion where I want it to go.

1   2   3   4   5   6   7   8   9   10

I negotiate in a style that I feel is compatible with the style of negotiating in the country where I am doing business.

1   2   3   4   5   6   7   8   9   10

I try to keep overt conflict from occurring during a negotiation when all players are present, and deal with the issue later, perhaps through a third party.

1   2   3   4   5   6   7   8   9   10

I carefully watch the gestures and expressions of my negotiating counterparts as signals of their true feelings and reactions.

1   2   3   4   5   6   7   8   9   10

I try to deepen the business relationship during a negotiation rather than think only about closing the deal; I believe that to do so allows me to influence the outcome of the transaction.

1   2   3   4   5   6   7   8   9   10

Part II: Assessing Your Company for Negotiating Skills

My company feels that its negotiating approach must be customized for every country with which it does business.

1   2   3   4   5   6   7   8   9   10

My company tries to maintain the same group of negotiators on a deal throughout the bargaining process and beyond, to provide as much continuity to the relationship as possible.

1   2   3   4   5   6   7   8   9   10

My firm emphasizes hierarchy in its global negotiating teams; each person knows exactly what his/her role is during a bargaining session, and what level of status and seniority she/he has on the team.

1   2   3   4   5   6   7   8   9   10

My company has made an effort to educate its engineers and technicians about how to gather technical information from foreign clients, and how to control the flow of proprietary know-how to foreign clients.

1   2   3   4   5   6   7   8   9   10

My company seeks long-term and "relationship-oriented" partnerships with its overseas customers and suppliers, rather than short-term transactions based purely on the "bottom line."

1   2   3   4   5   6   7   8   9   10

As before, add up your score for each section of this quiz. If you or your firm scores 25 or lower out of a possible total of 50, the area of negotiating skills should be a key priority for you and your company.

Maintaining Global Ethics and Integrity

Many Americans think that their own business ethics are global. But in reality, there are different systems of business ethics—some existing in a formative state, others sophisticated; some based on religious precepts, others founded on ancient customary social organization. But all are different from American business ethics. Islamic ethics and mores, adhered to by one billion people worldwide (according to the Islamic Center in Washington, D.C.), are based on strict social obligations to honor parents, to show hospitality to in-group members as well as outsiders, to adhere to strict codes of sexual conduct and social interaction (stressing modest dress for women and separation of men and women in many settings), and to actively participate in religious occasions. America can hardly call itself the standard bearer for international business ethics. Standards of ethics are simply not universal.

Doing business through informal "backdoor" connections rather than through the local Thomas Register and based on who offers the lowest price goes against American notions of fairness. Finding the "fruitful connection," says Mr. Abdul Sheikh, an East African lawyer who has represented U.S. firms there, is absolutely critical for achieving business success in the countries of southern Africa and Nigeria. So, too, entrenched producer-distributor relationships based on *guanxi* (backdoor) connections represent a formidable obstacle to marketing foreign products in Greater China. In the PRC, in fact, the entire economic system of supply and demand is based on an informal distribution network. The monetary value of goods is often subordinate to the clout one has in terms of *guanxi* relationships. These relationships form the backbone of decision making, promotions, and resource allocation in China. Americans feel uncomfortable engaging in reciprocal favor performing and back scratching, which to them seems far outside the purview of commerce; unfortunately, for most of the world it is not.

Often, in order to sell products and services in emerging world markets, you have to enter paternalistic relationships with customers in which sellers cultivate buyers by providing extensive after-sales service. This too goes against the moral grain for Americans. In Japan, for example, and increasingly in Korea and other parts of the world, the customer is not only king, but God. Sellers are even thought to be of lower status than buyers, treated not as equals but as loyal allies of buyers; in return, buyers may watch out for sellers when times get tough (e.g., ordering goods above market value, finding them new customers, and protecting them from foreign competitors). Paternalistic buyer-seller bonds are hard to break, especially when you are a newcomer in a market. You have to offer more than just the lowest price. Unwillingness to accept the lower status position of suppliers and enter into paternalistic relationships with buyers is a primary reason, though not the sole reason, that American executives often hear their global customers say, "We will contact you when we are prepared to buy."

Unorthodox accounting and taxation practices also drive Americans up a wall overseas. In countries such as Spain, Taiwan, and Brazil it's common for companies to keep three sets of accounting books as a method to avoid taxes. A major U.S. beverage company recently purchased one of its offshore franchises back and found out that the owner (in Brazil) had falsified his tax returns for the previous two years. The U.S. firm informed the Brazilian that the U.S. company would be forced to engage the Brazilian government and refile the Brazilian's tax returns. The U.S. company was very willing to pay the back-due taxes, but felt that the Brazilian seller should know they were going to move in this way. As the U.S.

executive involved described it: "The Brazilian guy thought we were absolutely nuts because [he said] 'all Brazilian companies do this,' and 'Brazilian companies rarely include certain items'—besides the fact that he might get into trouble. He truly believed that we were crazy to take the time, effort, and expense to refile. But we absolutely did anyway."

Finally, and perhaps most disturbing to Westerners doing business in emerging markets, is the nonsanctity of legal contracts. Deals should stick, thinks the Westerner, and not be rewritten with each change in circumstances for the partner, as Koreans, Chinese, and Japanese often think they should. "A card laid is a card played." But in business cultures that put a priority on long-term relationships rather than the bottom-line outcome from a single agreement, negotiation is often followed by renegotiation. Interestingly, Asian negotiators often define "principles" of agreement between parties before formal negotiations open. One principle in China is typically that the foreign party will "contribute to mutual cooperation and the modernization of China." The legalistic American agrees haphazardly, thinking his affirmation is nonbinding since it's not in the final contract. Then, when circumstances become difficult for the Chinese, they often remind the foreigner that he should repair the situation (at significant added cost to him) because he "had agreed to do everything in his power to assist in China's modernization."

Americans are not just legally prevented from influencing foreign buyers and governments in an unorthodox manner, but many are ethically unable to do so. Other activities that challenge our ethical code might include spending a night on the town with Thai clients that includes a sex show or gambling with Macao business partners. Such business-related practices tend to violate the Westerner's internalized sense of integrity. And this is the way it should be: "What you have to ask yourself," admonishes Rabbi Wayne Dosick, a business ethicist, "is what's right and what's wrong. There are different penalties for what's right and what's wrong. But right and wrong remain. It's you who has to sleep with yourself at night."

Should we adjust our ethics? Andrew Young said in 1978 that "nothing is illegal if one hundred businessmen decide to do it." The notion of cultural relativism embodied in this statement suggests that ethics vary depending on the values held by unique cultures. Something considered unethical in one place may not be looked upon as unethical in another. In many places, for example, bribery is considered in the same light as tipping is here—rewarding someone for service rendered. In emerging economies, bribery is how a vast number of people eke out a living. It's not thought of as corruption any more than expecting a tip is thought of as a corrupt act here. It's built into the economic system of many countries. As international business spreads into emerging markets, however, the safe haven of cultural relativism has lost ground fast to new, universal codes of ethics and mores, especially in regard to standards concerning child labor, human rights, and protecting the environment.

Creating Your Firm's—and Your Own—Code of Conduct

Every company needs to know exactly where it stands on a gamut of ethical issues, and needs to know before it sends people overseas. Employees need to know exactly what they can and cannot do. Otherwise, they will be left stranded and at risk of getting into serious trouble.

Design an international code of ethics rather than one for each country in which you do business. Align the overseas code of conduct with your domestic code as much as possible. Erring on the side of clarity is better than erring on the side of vagueness. If the policy is vague, people may get into compromising positions. Gray areas should be defined as well. The firm may prefer not to engage in certain practices, but its representatives can be instructed to look for creative solutions. Contacts within the company can be defined for these situations. The guidelines cannot be allowed to collect dust in the bottom drawers of the desks of your overseas people. Take heed from "Snow White," also known as Big Blue. IBM's "Business Conduct Guidelines" must be read by salespeople and key personnel in the field at least once a year (and they must sign off to that effect).

Before venturing anywhere overseas, you must also figure out where you personally stand on all of the ethical issues discussed here. Enter the business relationship with your ethical thresholds well defined. Whether you are conservative or liberal, if you are clear on these issues, being consistent in your behavior will win you respect. Know where you can, and cannot, compromise your ethics. Know where you can, and cannot, be flexible. More than anything, you don't want to let yourself get caught in a situation where you've done something you feel uncomfortable about and the customer knows it. In short, have a personal code of ethics and sign a contract with yourself to ensure that you personally enforce it.

A World of Gifts, Graft, and Bribes

In no country is bribery officially sanctioned or condoned. Nonetheless, in many countries bribery forms a fulcrum between what is proper and ethical and what is sometimes necessary for business and making a profit. In some countries you can fairly say that there has always been a custom of greasing the palm, and it isn't considered immoral or unethical. In Thailand and Indonesia, if you want to get a driver's license or obtain a business permit, you pay an agent. In Nigeria, you pay the customs agent to get out of the airport. In the United States, we pay fees to do all of these things, but the money goes to government bureaucracies, lawyers, freight forwarders, and documentation services. In the Philippines, Vietnam, and elsewhere, many of these institutionalized charges don't exist yet. Instead, they are handled by informal payments to a legion of facilitators. In Indonesia, for example, so-called commercial corruption has been an integral part of the culture for a very long time, and at every level of the society—from the vendor on the street to the president's office—to such a degree that President Suharto's wife has long been nicknamed Madame TienPercent!

Not-so-petty corruption has permeated East European societies. While *apparatchiks* (officials) were part of the educated elite, they usually earned a lower salary than their private-sector counterparts. Thus, informal barter and favor giving were important supplements to regular modes of commerce. The system was common even in the medical profession, where doctors were historically underpaid. If you didn't tip the surgeon, you might not get your operation. Nowadays, especially in the former Soviet republics, "you can't get anything without bribes," as a private store director complained to a "bribery hot-line" in Russia run by the newspaper *Komsomolskaya Pravda.* He said, "I get a delivery of cigarettes—10 percent goes to the . . . distributor. Looking for space for your store? That'll be 10 grand on top."

As officials in newly opened private economies, they are still underpaid, and sometimes they drag their feet unless motivated with cash. Third World government officials, many of whom control some of the world's largest infrastructure projects, are typically educated elites who are grossly undersalaried relative to their counterparts in industry, a prime motive for dipping into the till. A retired British executive, quoted in the *Wall Street Journal,* described the current situation like this: "Five percent of $200,000 will be interesting to a senior official. . . . Five percent of $200 million justifies the serious attention of the head of state."

The Americans who represent Fortune 500 companies in Vietnam, for example, find themselves in a terrible position vis-à-vis their competition, because Vietnamese business culture puts a premium on gift giving and what is really flat-out bribery, including cash, women, and free trips to Las Vegas and Epcot Center. Here's a typical dilemma. The local People's Committee wants $10,000 in cash to approve your hotel project in Danang, on the central coast of Vietnam. If you don't pay it, you might find that your hotel gets built but has plastic pipes for plumbing. So do you pay the $10,000 now, or do you pay $4 million later to tear the whole thing down and start all over again? The U.S. representative wants desperately to pay the $10,000 now, however morally repugnant it might be, rather than have the project fail in the long run. The parent company wants to keep its nose clean and abide by U.S. law. The Americans there live tortured lives: Do they follow the law and perhaps their ethical instincts, or do they compete against the Japanese and Singaporeans and everyone else who's soliciting business in Vietnam, the new tiger economy of Asia?

A former trade negotiator admitted that regarding illicit payments, our rigid antibribery laws "put our businesspeople in a difficult position." The United States has legislated the most restrictive antibribery laws in the world, while many of its competitors enforce no restrictions at all; Italian, German, Dutch, and Japanese firms are not only permitted to use bribery to influence overseas entities, they can deduct the value of the bribe from their taxes as a necessary business expense! Recently, the Clinton administration urged the 26-nation Organization for Economic Cooperation and Development (OECD) to form a committee to write U.S.-like antibribery legislation to be enforced by industrial countries around the world. Nothing doing, however. "We cannot accept . . . the recommendation somewhat obliging Japan to change its criminal-law system," said a foreign ministry official in Tokyo. European countries have voiced objections as well.

Harbo Jensen of Chevron admits that his company "loses business in several countries because we will not [pay bribes]." He says that all U.S. companies are at a disadvantage compared to foreign companies in tying up crude supplies out of certain countries. Jensen says Chevron's no-bribery policy is in place for two reasons: first, he says, "it's the law and we don't break the law" and second, "we have a certain corporate image; we're one of those companies that posts its values on the walls." At Hughes Space and Communications Company, "it's company policy that we do not participate in those kinds of activities," says division administration manager Karen Rakita, "which seems to put us at a disadvantage at times, but it's flat out—we don't pay."

These statements are not to be chalked up to mere public relations verbiage. In countries that are trying to reduce bureaucratic corruption (as Vietnam has recently and Mexico did six years ago), Western companies with a clean bill of ethical health have an advantage. Reform-minded governments seek partnerships with large firms they know will not be prone to pay local officials kickbacks. "A foreign government decides that it wants to clean up its act," says Jensen. "They'll appoint someone to head the national oil company, or the national oil company will decide to begin to privatize. When this change comes, the president of such an organization, employing, say, 4,000 people, doesn't want to have to be looking over everyone's shoulder making sure they keep their hands out of the till." By doing business with Chevron, they know their employees are probably not doing something under the table. "Thus we think our policy gives us an advantage," says Jensen. "We lose many more deals than we gain by our sense of honesty. But that's a sacrifice we're willing to make."

Moreover, locals often resent the fact that foreign firms provide big-dollar bribes, which drives up the price of goods and services for local companies that can't afford to dole out such bribes. This fuels resentment against Western firms known to make bribes, while polishing the image of those firms that do not.

You must be on your toes, however, about anticorruption regimes in foreign countries. Mexico ratified strong anticorruption laws at the outset of the Salinas presidential term, but local agents contrived to inform U.S. businesses that paying a *"mordida"* (Spanish for "bite") is necessary to win a contract in Mexico. One of the authors represented Science Applications International Corporation (SAIC) in Mexico and experienced this problem firsthand when his counterpart liaison in Mexico informed him that the Mexican consulate representative in San Diego would "provide all the necessary introductions for the deal in exchange for 10 percent of the deal." Would a Mexican consulate official working inside the United States behave in so blatant a manner with an unfamiliar marketing company wanting to sell airport equipment in Mexico? Of course not. The agent was bilking the foreign supplier.

Some countries have attempted to eradicate commercial corruption, while others seem to accept it. To be sure, whether or not the government wants to dispel it often has little effect. Mike Lorelli of Pizza Hut admits, "There are times where you can't hide behind the Foreign Corrupt Practices Act, because what you perceive as a violation is merely part of their culture, and has been for a long time." In these business cultures, he says, bribery is "not viewed as being wrong any more than us tipping a cabby." Lorelli adds, "In the Middle East or Brazil, they would think you are crazy for not offering a bribe, because to them there is absolutely nothing wrong with bribery. You're an oddball, but there's not a thing you can do about it."

Should your company do as the Romans do? (Or do as your competition does?) You and your company need to consider this ethical dilemma carefully. Since its inception, Hughes Space and Communications Company has sold a sizable percentage of products overseas. Bill Pomeranz, who has worked in the business group for 29 years as a business manager in charge of price, costing, and negotiations, says, "There were two instances where Hughes lost contracts because of little white envelopes or because we refused to pay heads of government or their deputies. And that's okay." But, says Pomeranz, "Hughes is blessed; we are the market leader and we have the ability to offer more than any other company, including those that would make payoffs."

This is a key fact of international commercial life: if you are clearly the best, you won't have to contend with having to bribe officials to beat out the competition. If you are selling a product that is absolutely critical to the buying country's development, then you can get away with maintaining a hard-line attitude about bending your ethical code to suit local conditions. Chevron's code of business conduct unequivically states: "While in some instances payments [of a corrupt nature] may be acceptable in the country where made, they are strictly against our policy even though the refusal to make them may cause the company to lose business."

Some U.S. companies decide to do as the Romans do. A representative of IBM in a Southeast Asian country told us the following: "A wrong tactic here would be to go in saying you're not paying commissions to anyone on this deal because in the United States we don't pay commissions to a middleman. Here, it's standard to pay a commission to a middleman. Much of your business is done through a third party. Such a practice is not considered illegal. You hire a consultant or a business adviser to help you do it. There are agents for virtually everything because it is difficult to get things done. Then you as a person do not have to worry about how they get it done; you are not a party to it. You are hiring him to perform a service. If he has to pay people, that's his prerogative."

Asked why Hughes took a hard line against playing by local rules, Pomeranz summed up the feelings of many Fortune 500 firms: "It's illegal. Whether it's the way somebody would want to do business or not, it's illegal—and the company has a rigid code of ethics that prohibits unlawful conduct." You must know what is illegal and what isn't before you or your company thinks about paying commissions to independent agents or fixers.

The Foreign Corrupt Practices Act

Mike Lorelli offered this advice: "The first thing people working for an American multinational firm have to do is familiarize themselves with the Foreign Corrupt Practices Act. That's first—before you have your business card printed and before you get on a plane for anywhere." Without studying for the next bar exam, let's take a look at the Foreign Corrupt Practices Act. When you're next confronted by a midlevel ministry official with hat in hand, you'll be happy you did.

The investigations related to Watergate blew apart the nexus of massive, worldwide commissions being paid by U.S. corporations. Archibald Cox wanted to know more about large sums of cash payments by U.S. corporations into the secret coffers of their favored politicians. The subpoenaed records of Lockheed and Northrop revealed enormous payments to a long list of fixers, including Adnan Khashoggi, Prince Bernhard of the Netherlands, high-echelon members of the Italian government, and Japanese Premier Kakuei Tanaka. "Bribing was wholesale," recalls William Proxmire, the author of the bill, when he looks back on the early 1970s.[1]

Hundreds of international companies were making huge payoffs around the world; offering kickbacks and pledging cash gifts were nothing less than a critical component in a company's competitive advantage overseas. A. Carl Kotchian, the president of Lockheed from 1965 until 1977, expressed the collective sentiments of multinational firms up until the Foreign Corrupt Practices Act was passed: "I knew that if we wanted our product to have a chance to win on its own merits, we had to follow the functioning system [in Japan]. If we wanted our product to have a chance, we understood that we would have to pay, or pledge to pay, substantial sums of money in addition to the contractual sales commissions. We never *sought* to make these extra payments. We would have preferred not to have the additional expense for the sale. But, always, they were recommended by those whose experience and judgment we trusted and whose recommendations we therefore followed."[2]

In his defense after the Multinational Hearings of 1975, Mr. Khashoggi said, "When I approach the Saudi government on your behalf, the money that you pay me is my commission. In Arabia it is honorable for you to give and for me to receive the money. It is only if I offer it to the government servant, and he accepts it, that it becomes a bribe."[3] As regards U.S. law, he's right; but how much of the total of $154 million that Lockheed and its competitor, Northrop, paid him in commissions ended up being transferred to Arab officials in the form of gifts, use of his private planes, and stakes in unrelated deals? Only Mr. Khashoggi knows for sure. Would such gifts be legal under the current reading of the Foreign Corrupt Practices Act? Undoubtedly they would not.

The Foreign Corrupt Practices Act "prohibits U.S. businesses from paying bribes openly or using middlemen as conduits for a bribe when the U.S. official knows that part of the middleman's payment will be used as a bribe."[4] Though the Act does not apply directly to non-U.S. subsidiaries of U.S. companies, the government has made it clear "that if a non-U.S. subsidiary engages in transactions prohibited by these provisions, they will attempt to prosecute the parent corporation and its officers and employees who know or should have known about the transactions."[5]

You might ask: What's the difference between paying a Washington lobbyist to bend the ears of congressmen to help you win a contract and paying a liaison like Khashoggi to facilitate a deal? There is no difference legally unless Mr. Khashoggi shared some of the money that you paid him with Saudi government officials to facilitate the deal.

Bribes, kickback, grease, commissions, payoffs, baksheesh—whatever you want to call it—take three basic forms, all of which are encompassed in the Act.

• *Lubrication* refers to relatively small amounts of cash paid to lower-level government officials for the purpose of expediting their normal duties.

• *Subornation* entails the payment of a large sum of cash to an official to commit an illegal act on behalf of the briber.

• *Agents* make it easier for money to change hands. The seller puts in place a middleman, who is paid for services rendered in generating introductions, coordinating meetings, and acting as a go-between. Paying a third party to undertake these tasks is legal, just like paying a real estate agent to locate a property for sale—

that is, unless the agent uses some of the money paid by the U.S. company to bribe government officials.

Violating the Act can cost your firm up to $2 million in fines, $100,000 for individuals, and imprisonment of perpetrators for up to five years. But there's a catch: Depending on how closely you read the Act and how you interpret it, the law could apply only to paying or giving a gift to an official to do something outside the normal course of his or her capacity. During the peak of her career, for example, Imelda Marcos was the governor of Metropolitan Manila. She had the final approval for all municipal projects in that district. If you were involved as a foreign contractor in the construction of a Metro Manila project and you wanted to expedite the approval of something she had control over in the normal course of her official duties, depending on how you read the Act, it could be deemed legal to bribe Imelda Marcos. Now, if you wanted to build a hotel in Makati and approval fell outside the purview of Imelda and you bribed her in exchange for the influence she could bear on getting the deal approved, you would be in direct violation of the Foreign Corrupt Practices Act. To be safe from a strict interpretation of the Act, you would not bribe Imelda at all, without getting the opinion of about five good lawyers.

The Enlightened Corporation

When a supplier of lobster in Honduras fails to provide its divers with safety gear and is seriously depleting the coastal lobster population, is the American company buying the lobster responsible? The company in question claims it's only a buyer of lobster and has no role in the protection of local workers or the Honduras environment. The company says its business provides the poor of the area with the means to raise their standard of living. Growing numbers of people are asking, however, Where does the buck stop?

While multinational firms were viewed during the 1970s as a force for peace in the world, antagonism against them has grown since the late 1980s in response to their ill effects on the planet and its inhabitants. From the point of view of developing nations, global firms are enormous organisms. Many rightly fear their bigness and their concentration of power. As our companies go global, our corporate responsibilities must internationalize as well.

Multinational corporations have been charged, at various times, with supporting repressive governments, polluting the environment, selling untested pharmaceuticals and unsafe factory equipment, depleting natural resources, and abusing Third World labor. "In the latter days of the century," writes Gary Cohen of the *Third World Network,* "the global corporation has emerged as the predominant agent of destruction, with an ideology that condones the sacrifice of people and the planet at the altar of free trade and next quarter's profit margin." Many people would concur.

Does it have to be so?

In their book *Global Dreams,* Richard Barnet and John Cavanagh concluded, after extensive interviews with executives of multinational firms around the world, that the vast majority of global corporations find social and political concerns beyond their control, and outside their role.[6] Barnet told us in no uncertain terms: "The global outlook of the [international] company is strictly related to the character of the markets, knowledge about how to take advantage of the international traffic in money, and the notion that their clientele is global. The most one can expect from a corporation is that it understand both the limits and the weight of legal sanctions not to act contrary to the public interest."

With the proliferation of regimes across the globe, however, corporations must be more consciously moral in pursuing their business objectives. Global corporations believe that local governments are responsible for legislating worker safety rules, child labor laws, and environmental protection regulations, but the dependence of local governments on foreign business allows for such policies to be easily vulgarized by irresponsible firms. The role of the corporation should be to support and empower local governments in institutionalizing commercial ground rules and codes of conduct. Not to do so will expose firms to the wrath of local governments and their populations, not to mention the international press. The sooner MNCs unite and form the international regimes that can enforce acceptable modes of global commercial endeavor and impel foreign governments to adhere to basic conditions of human rights, the sooner they can expect to avoid the negative effects of public outcry and negative press. The profit motive implies taking every advantage that you can. There is little short-term incentive for a single corporate player to behave unilaterally and globally in a thoughtful, fair, conscientious manner. Most firms wait to be compelled to behave morally.

As industrialization advanced in the nineteenth century, some efforts were made by the world's developed countries to protect labor and resources, and in the twentieth century, similar efforts were made to restrict monopolies. The global public can be expected eventually to do the same, unless multinational firms forge collective consensus and lead the way. Says University of California sociology professor Harvey Goldman, "If companies don't take that initiative, international regimes are probably going to take some of those steps. The question is: Will corporations be proactive or wait for that to happen and fight it tooth and nail?" Our notion is that they can get ahead of the curve and thus be even more attractive to the countries that seek foreign investment. They can take more of a lead now in participating collectively in solving the world's problems rather than being blamed for them.

Why be a good corporate citizen with a sense of morality? Quite simply, because host countries are more willing to grant preferential treatment to firms that look out for workers, protect resources, share technology, and so on. Says Matsushita's Ronn Richard: "We're known to be good corporate citizens, and that helps a lot. If we go to Mexico and they're worried about our pollution standards, we can say, 'Look at other Third World countries like Thailand and China where we have factories and go see that we're light-years ahead of all the local companies in terms of how we treat the environment.' "

A Creed for Twenty-first-Century Capitalism

If it hasn't already done so, your firm needs to create its own moral charter for global expansion. This is different from an overseas code of conduct or ethics. It encapsulates your global corporate standards and business philosophy—a set of guiding principles to be followed by all affiliates whether they are located on Madison Avenue or in the Amazon jungle. The standards you uphold at home should be those you uphold everywhere.

Matsushita's is perhaps the most famous corporate charter in the history of commerce. Says Ronn Richard, "We operate here under what we call the Basic Business Principles. It's a little book that everybody gets when they join the company; it's the company creed." He reads from the booklet: "The ultimate purpose of any business enterprise should be to make people's lives richer and happier, thereby helping to bring peace and prosperity to society."

The following principles, however, will at least make it likely that you'll avoid the public outcry against many global firms.

"Wherever We Do Business in the World, We Do So with the Attitude of a 'Corporate Guest' "

Pursue profits while taking responsibility for long- and short-term impact on the community of man. Firms need to maintain an openness to new business opportunities while retaining a ground-level sensitivity to sociopolitical concerns. As the "new kid on the block" in a foreign business community, public relations needs to be a top priority.

First, try to expand your personal network of contacts inside *and* *outside* the foreign business community in a given country. Work to get the venture accepted into the community as a local, rather than a foreign firm. Ways you can readily accomplish this are to:

- Attend trade shows and conferences.
- Join trade and industrial associations.
- Publish a company newsletter announcing employee accomplishments, R&D activities, and expansion plans.
- Sponsor community events and recreational activities.
- Sponsor grass-roots environmentalism.

Second, develop your image without being ostentatious. Invest in local philanthropic projects as much as you do Madison Avenue image making. The press can be highly influential in emerging markets, and you will want to engage with it whenever possible. For example, after 40 years of anticapitalist, anti-West propaganda in the former Soviet bloc, smart companies from the West try to counter that by conducting constant public relations. R. J. Reynolds Tobacco International president Dale Sisel handed over a $100,000 check to its new joint venture partner in St. Petersburg to train managers at a new school and to "show our new neighbors in this city that we will try to make life for our workers here, and in the whole city overall, better." IBM has donated computers to a Russian Orthodox church; and after winning a multibillion dollar oil exploration contract, McDermott shipped in humanitarian aid by air and sea to Sakhalin Island.

"We Pursue Long-Term Involvements with Host Countries"

The mobility of companies and their increasing incentive to move from country to country works to the detriment of host nations and their populations. Nike goes to Korea until wages go up and then moves to Indonesia. Now, the Indonesian government worries that Nike is going to pack up and go to Vietnam. Malaysia shudders that the flotilla of foreign semiconductor manufacturers that have utilized cheap skilled labor in that country are soon going to load up and exit en masse to India, where labor is cheaper and English-speaking. The days of multinational firms hopscotching from country to country seeking low-cost labor seem to be ending, however, as local consumer markets blossom and the price of exiting a country and returning is high.

Be a long-term partner. This makes for sound global strategy and is attractive to the host country. If you don't reinvest in the local economy where you use cheaper labor to manufacture something, you delay the development of a local market to which you could eventually sell manufactured goods and services. In the end you sabotage your own company. Consider your move into a new country as a permanent involvement. It may begin by taking advantage of cheap labor but should progress through ascending levels of engagement to a point where all of the activities we've mentioned as strategies are being pursued simultaneously, from manufacturing for export to conducting R&D in the country. If your firm must pack up and leave a country, make sure it leaves the country better off for your having been there.

"We Do No Harm to the Earth's Environment"

We are all responsible for safeguarding the planet, especially in areas where lax controls have resulted in irreparable damage to the earth's environment. It is simply not in the long-term interest of your firm to be exporting filth to countries or locating in countries to take advantage of lax environmental laws. Nothing more clearly undermines the power of national governments to regulate their own environment and the grass-roots effort to lengthen the life of the planet. The world's environmental scorecard gets worse every year.

Be as conscious of environmental responsibilities overseas as you would be in the United States. If you don't help an emerging country sustain its environment, you will be blamed later, possibly shunned by the country as a business partner, and suffer immense damage to your firm's image, much as Union Carbide did after the Bhopal accident and Exxon after its oil spill in Alaska. Your company's ethical code should state categorically that should it damage the local environment, it will be responsible for cleaning up—with no equivocation. It should, on a continual basis, decrease the use of materials that threaten endangered species or flora and fauna, or threaten the purity of the local water supply.

Two American utility companies—Niagara Mohawk and Arizona Public Service—recently traded pollution rights in a deal that signals a growing trend. A company is given permission by state and national agencies to pollute up to a certain level; if it doesn't use those rights or doesn't pollute as much as permitted, a firm can sell or trade such rights to another firm, which may not have been granted rights, or has used up its quota. The precedent opens the way for firms to buy, transfer, and trade rights to pollute the planet. Niagara Mohawk was even more innovative, and more global. The utilities simply "donated" pollution rights and, in exchange, received tax breaks. The saved revenue will be spent on trying out new ways to reduce emissions in countries like China and Russia, where lax controls provide cheap cleanup opportunities. Can we expect global speculators to invest in pollution rights (as they might media time) with the intention of trading those rights on the open world market? It sounds insidious, but such a development might help to restrict total pollution of our air and waterways by "marketizing" conservation practices.

"We Uphold Universal Labor Standards"

Virtually every nation is desperately trying to attract global companies to put more of their unemployed to work. Any meddlesome regulations in this area are considered to only work against a nation's competitiveness. The Indonesian government, for example, recently cracked down on its incipient labor movement—beating and jailing demonstrators and closing down two prominent newspapers covering the events—in its effort to stifle calls for worker protection and raise wages. President Suharto, one can surmise, wants to allay fears on the part of foreign investors that their plants might become the target of strikes or unionization. The AFL-CIO has had little success in mobilizing governments or local unions, in Indonesia and elsewhere, to ratify laws concerning the rights and wages of global workers.

Here again, it is up to enlightened corporations to make the difference. There should be a commitment on the part of your firm to raise labor standards wherever your firm goes; that is, it should not support, but indeed should oppose, political restraints on what might be called a free labor market, the intimidation of workers, or the denial of rights to bargain collectively. Why? Because this has an effect on working conditions and labor in your home country; if you allow your contractor to use sweatshop labor there, you encourage sweatshop labor at home. This cuts demand and jeopardizes prospects for growth of buying power among overseas consumers. And raising labor standards will keep your employee turnover down and productivity rising.

A "fair" wage may be impossible to define; paying a Chinese worker five dollars a day may sound immoral, until one considers that that wage is double the average wage of China's 800 million peasants. In a case where five dollars a day would not provide a worker with enough income to subsist with dignity as a human being, then the employer can, and should, be criticized as immoral. Note, however, that global firms in developing economies are often criticized by local firms for paying higher than local wages, thus making it difficult for local employers to attract and keep skilled workers. In such conditions the firm should offer at least a subsistence wage, and help workers to form organizations that will protect their interests.

To utilize another country's cheap labor is one thing, but to abuse its workers is quite another. What are appropriate *universal* labor laws, beyond wage level? How many total days per week, and how many hours per day, should a worker be asked to toil? And with what assurance of basic safety? What should the minimum age of workers be? You dignify your overseas people by looking out for their well-being just as attentively as you might your domestic people. What assurances can you provide your people that they and their families are being looked after? Is it time to set up "care management" functions in the overseas enterprise (e.g., flextime, in-house day care, and after-school programs) before the union or local government forces you to do so? All this will generate loyalty and unity among your people.

Whether or not the central government in a country supports intraenterprise unions and associations, your firm should, and do so overtly. China, for instance, has never been friendly to independent trade unions, but it sees that unions are forming within its borders as foreign investors set up thousands of factories. Most of the violations committed by foreign firms against workers in China are committed by other Asian companies doing business there. Western companies doing business in the region should encourage their Asian subsidiaries to allow for and encourage the formation of independent unions representing the interests of workers in their factories in China and elsewhere.

"We Share Know-how and Appropriate Technology Overseas"

In the global era, knowledge will become synonymous with economic power and greatly determine the ability of a nation to improve the circumstances of its people. National programs for building information technologies are popping up everywhere—from the Japanese Fifth Generation projects, the European ESPRIT project, and the Alvey project in the United Kingdom, to Malaysia's Vision 2020. Even Vietnam has a policy called IT 2000, for urgently building up its science and technology infrastructure. In the global century, access to applied knowledge and technology is clearly the ticket to long-term growth, wealth creation, and modernization. We have noted already that the world is fast becoming divided into technology haves and have-nots. The disparity grows worse as most of the formal technology transfer between the developed and the undeveloped world has been organization-sponsored (UN, World Bank, and OECD) rather than transfer from multinational firms to developing countries.

Again, corporations can do something to help.

For starters, a firm's global network of partnerships should not be marked by technology haves and have-nots. Technology transfer is not complete until the recipient company has assimilated the technology, not just for manufacturing products but also for bettering the product and designing new products based on its own innovation. The bottom-line benefits of this approach are clear. Following the examples of South Korea, Taiwan, and China, emerging countries offer benefits—like market access and tax breaks—in exchange for technology, training, and know-how. Comparator Systems Corporation of Newport Beach, California, has proposed as part of their joint venture package with a partner in Malaysia to bring to R&D-poor Malaysia some of the world's leading scientists who consult with Comparator. These scientists, says CEO Robert Rogers, "would love to work in virgin territory like Malaysia and help train a whole new class of students who really want to do basic research." His willingness to assist Malaysia in technological modernization won him a personal meeting with Prime Minister Mahatir during his second visit to the country, a meeting his corporate friends tell him they have been working at getting for years. Conversely, firms that set up in these nations and black-box their technology while minimizing the sharing of their know-how will be labeled unattractive partners, much as Japanese firms were in China during the 1980s.

As opposed to merely selling advanced technology, the global company must also be able to *transfer* technology. The right questions must be answered in preliminary feasibility studies so that the technology transferred is such that the recipient can assimilate effectively. Huge losses are sustained when Western companies don't check and recheck assurances concerning power and water supply, for example, or when they agree to sell state-of-the-art equipment (because the recipient demands it), knowing full well that such equipment is not going to function properly in that environment. The savvy firm ensures that its technical people receive cross-cultural training and that its cross-cultural negotiators understand essential aspects of the technology.

"We Do No Harm to Indigenous Cultures"

We are all part of an emerging, more integrated global society, but racial, ethnic, religious, national, and cultural diversity will always be the rule among humankind. We live in two worlds at once: our home cultures and that of world culture. And no people should be asked to abandon any part of their culture. Every people of every culture must be honored as unique and worth protecting. With MNCs and their executives guided by a spirit of coexistence with different peoples, especially minority indigenous people, they can be a critical factor in preserving the ethnic diversity left on earth instead of being a cause of its destruction. During this century, according to the United Nations, 2,000 different peoples— not species of flora and fauna, mind you, but peoples—were lost forever to extinction. In many instances the demise of these peoples was at the hands of executive decision makers of multinational firms.

Some native groups with the stamina and cohesion to rebel are doing so. Indigenous communities around the world are demanding, and getting, more accountability from foreign companies. Their combined actions coupled with the growing support they receive from international organizations has forced U.S. oil companies in Russia, for example, to provide medical supplies and to build low-cost housing for former Soviet soldiers returning from Eastern Europe. Native groups in Papua New Guinea have won virtual veto power over energy projects proposed by foreign companies there.

Many Western companies have become sensitized to the issue and have made adjustments to lessen the impact of their activities on local cultures. Maxus Energy Corporation, for example, operates what it says is the largest heavy oil development project on the planet in Coca, Ecuador. To maintain good relations with the indigenous Waotrani natives, Maxus pays native men to protect the forest skirting the road into the field, has sponsored a school, and has funded a project to inventory plants removed in clearing the 80-foot-wide road leading to its fields as well as one to grow native species for reforestation. The company claims that 5 to 10 percent of the project's total budget is earmarked to cover environmental and social costs.

"We Help to Close the Gap Between the World's Rich and Poor"

The human population of the world lives on either side of a global Grand Canyon. The economic disparity between nations is staggering. While Japan's annual per capita gross domestic product is $29,000, Sweden's $32,600, and Germany's $27,900, Nigeria's is only $278, Vietnam's $200, and Mali's a numbing $83. The richest one-sixth of the planet's population controls five-sixths of its wealth. By the turn of the century, over a billion people will live in poverty. "As happened at the start of the industrial revolution," writes Alvin Toffler, "millions find their incomes threatened, their ways of work obsolete, their futures uncertain, their power slashed."[7]

Global class divisions have widened. Small English-speaking elite groups enjoy purchasing power while the majority is shut out. Entrepreneurs and local mafias dually control the private economies of the former Soviet Union and much of the former East bloc. "There are two parallel Moscows now," writes David Brooks in the

Wall Street Journal, "the red ruble Moscow of shortages and queues and the green dollar Moscow of high-octane gasoline and cellular phones." Only foreign currency will buy coveted imported goods, or those in short supply. Those who have green *bakks*—mostly *biznessmeni* and gangsters—hang out at the new casinos and discos watching the floor shows, while those earning in rubles pawn what they own on street corners to survive "shock therapy."

Only a decade ago it was a crime *not* to be employed in Soviet bloc countries. Now, joblessness in East Germany has reached two-thirds of the working population; more than a million Poles have lost their jobs, and in Hungary, one out of ten people have. One-third of all Russians now find themselves living below the poverty line. Increasing numbers of people around the world are in the informal economy that ranges from cutting hair at the side of the road in Saigon or selling lottery tickets in Mexico City to big-time criminal operations. Meanwhile, 47 million people enter the global labor pool each year.

How long will these emerging disenfranchised masses remain silent? What can be done? Part of taking more "responsibility for global profits" is watching out for emerging *people,* and not just the markets that they represent. Businesses everywhere can lead an effort to widen the playing field and increase the number of participants in global culture and commerce. Your mission statement should include the idea of building community and developing the skills of people, for the purpose of profiting as well as raising the standards of people's lives.

We don't mean to imply that your company's investment in an emerging nation does damage. We urge you only to recognize disparity and the social and political risk being created. While foreigners read publications that talk about the benefits of opening markets to foreign competition, the wisdom of rapid privatization, lower tariffs, and free trade agreements, foreign factories like Nissan's, Xerox's, and Texas Instruments' have turned Mexico's northern towns into enclaves of newly rich and newly poor. Slum inhabitants number 20,000 in Aguascalientes—double the number in 1990. Most of these people have migrated into the city and work in foreign companies at an average wage of $7 per day. Meanwhile, first-class residential areas grow to house the city's new business elite. Lend a hand in finding solutions.

"We Work to Strengthen Background Institutions on Behalf of Nation-States"

When arbitrager George Soros speculated on the British pound, and the pound fell, the notion that there is national control over local economies vanished. Every country is now, to a greater or lesser degree, held hostage to the world economy because of the trading of foreign currencies. (To their consternation, corporations likewise have no control over currency speculation, or currency values; over 90 percent of international foreign currency trading is unrelated to capital investment or trade.) To resist the forces of globally integrated capitalism is now impossible for even the most powerful nation states. When Mitterand came to power in France in 1981 and tried to nationalize businesses, raise wages, and take unilateral control of its currency rate, capital fled out of France so fast that within three years the country's socialists were heard advocating policies of integration with the European Community. To remain part of the world economy, the French were compelled to move more or less consistently with world economic demands.

It doesn't matter whether there are 7,000 global companies (as in the 1970s) or 35,000 (as in the 1990s) from the point of view of the nation-state. When companies avoid investing in a country based on rational commercial decisions, a nation-state loses control over the management and building of its economy. "[T]he message is clear," says Paul Kennedy. "If you do not follow the rules of the market, your economy will suffer."[8] Except for the largest and most powerful like the G7 countries, nation-states are not able to adequately protect their people from the harsh realities, unfairness, and injustices that being a weak player in the global trade war entails, and citizens are increasingly frustrated with their governments.

So-called international regimes are in vogue in international relations academia, a field of study that no longer deals with issues of "diplomacy," having replaced it with political economy—the movement of goods and capital, and the effects of a tremendously changed global economy on international politics. International regimes emerged initially in response to the destruction of the earth's environment. For example, Indian groups living in the rain forests of Ecuador have filed suit against Texaco in a U.S. district court in an attempt to force the firm to clean up its mess in its Amazon oil fields. The pressure being mounted against Texaco is well organized and assisted by international environmental organizations *outside* Ecuador, including the Natural Resources Defense Council, Oxfam America, and the Rainforest Action Network.[9] And the international regime concept is spreading into other areas of global concern, many of which are likely to affect the operations of multinational corporations.

Corporations should start now to actively participate directly with these nascent background organizations. Whether through funding or board membership, the foresighted global firm needs to become vigorously engaged with organizations and agencies geared to mobilizing public opinion and resources. Sooner or later, these regimes will have great influence on the globe's new regulatory environment, from pollution laws and fishing rights to product safety standards and corporate conduct. Companies need to take the lead both in supporting their efforts and in forming them, or pay the price later of being controlled by their initiatives without being involved in the process.

"We Uphold Basic Human Rights Wherever We Do Business"

The willingness of governments to force MNCs to avoid doing business with repressive countries has clearly waned as the importance of overseas commerce has grown. By decoupling most-favored-nation status for China in 1994, the Clinton administration struck a mortal blow to the idealistic notion that sanctions should be used to promote human rights in emerging nations. The United States has found that when it acts unilaterally, using its corporations as pawns to achieve leverage in the political sphere, it loses commercially and diplomatically. If forced to choose, America will choose to export its goods and services rather than its democratic freedom and human rights. This is partly due to America's economic decline relative to other industrial countries as well as feelings of international impotence. Concerns about human rights are continually overridden by concerns over the Germans, Koreans, and Japanese usurping emerging markets before us. Thus U.S. firms raced into Russia as Gorbachev mobilized forces against independence-seeking former republics, into India in disregard of its lax child labor laws and crackdowns on the politically restless in Kashmir and Punjab, into Indonesia in the face of protests of the AFL-CIO over the quashing of the country's labor movement and continuing abuses in the former Portuguese colony of East Timor, and into China in the months following the Tiananmen uprising. Ashutosh Varshney, a Harvard India expert, summed up the trend in commenting on the renewing of China's MFN status in 1994: "[T]he message is loud and clear: if American business gets strongly involved in a country, human rights takes second place or even less than that."[10]

As government backs off from policing human rights around the world, corporations need to step up their own efforts or risk backlash and blame. The initiative rests with the business statesman to do the right thing. Look at the demise of apartheid in South Africa. As early as 1985, international banks were initiating meetings with the outlawed African National Congress of South Africa to discuss their withdrawal from the country to protest the continuation of apartheid. While Ronald Reagan and Margaret Thatcher and United Nations ambassador Jeane Kirkpatrick held firm in their openly sympathetic support for the Botha government, Western bankers and other capitalists responded to their stockholders and recognized that apartheid could not be tolerated. In 1985, the chairman of Chase Manhattan bank, Willard Butcher, pulled his bank out of South Africa and generated a mass exodus of American banks from the country, including Bankers Trust, Bank of America, and Security Pacific. The rand plummeted and capital gushed out of the country.[11] In a globally integrated world, a firm's shareholders, depositors, and the public's attitude can impose sanctions on commercial activities without their government mandating it.

Corporations can do the right thing and still be profitable.

Part I: Assessing Yourself for Ethics and Integrity

Answer each item by circling the appropriate number on the continuum below:

To Almost No Extent		To Some Extent			To a Great Extent			To a Very Great Extent	
1	2	3	4	5	6	7	8	9	10

I enter an international business relationship aware of the ethical standards in my partner's country.

| 1 | 2 | 3 | 4 | 5 | 6 | 7 | 8 | 9 | 10 |

If (or when) I am confronted by a request to engage in what I consider unethical behavior, I respectfully decline rather than state that the activity is unethical or unlawful.

| 1 | 2 | 3 | 4 | 5 | 6 | 7 | 8 | 9 | 10 |

I have a clear understanding of the U.S Foreign Corrupt Practices Act.

| 1 | 2 | 3 | 4 | 5 | 6 | 7 | 8 | 9 | 10 |

I realize that when dealing in developing countries, I might need to write a contract that ensures success for both sides, rather than attempt to be clever and allow "the small print" to hinder my partner's interests.

| 1 | 2 | 3 | 4 | 5 | 6 | 7 | 8 | 9 | 10 |

I understand that the activities of my firm have an impact on people and communities overseas, whether positive or negative.

| 1 | 2 | 3 | 4 | 5 | 6 | 7 | 8 | 9 | 10 |

Part II: Assessing Your Company for Ethics and Integrity

My company understands that business ethics vary around the world and that, without going beyond what is legal under U.S. law, it must be sensitive and flexible when confronted by unfamiliar business practices overseas.

| 1 | 2 | 3 | 4 | 5 | 6 | 7 | 8 | 9 | 10 |

My company has written and distributed to all international staff a Code of Conduct manual covering issues such as gift giving, bribery, business entertaining, and international boycotts.

1   2   3   4   5   6   7   8   9   10

My company has made it clear to each member of its international staff that when confronted with an ethical dilemma overseas, he or she should contact a particular person or department at the company for advice on how to appropriately deal with the situation.

1   2   3   4   5   6   7   8   9   10

My company has made it clear to its overseas employees both the nature of the Foreign Corrupt Practices Act and how the company interprets and abides by it.

1   2   3   4   5   6   7   8   9   10

The executives at my company understand that as their firm expands globally, its responsibilities do also; they consider the social consequences of their international business decisions.

1   2   3   4   5   6   7   8   9   10

As before, add up your score for each section of this quiz. If you or your firm scores 25 or lower out of a possible total of 50, the area of ethics and integrity should be a key priority for you and your company.

STRATEGY VI

Taking Advantage of
Protocol Power

While "etiquette" may provoke quaint images of ladies' tea parties of yesteryear in America, this is far from the case in other parts of the globe. In fact, your intelligence, education, and status may be assessed by your manners, since these are thought to go hand in hand. It is for this reason that many corporations outside the United States invest highly in the ability of their employees to convey a good image to their partners and customers. Japanese corporations spend an estimated $700 million a year on outside etiquette training for their employees.

The word *etiquette* has its origins in a word that meant "a ticket that gained you the right of entry." Later it evolved to mean "something that marked someone and indicated their placement." In some ways, these definitions still hold true in a great many places: The ability to "act the part" is necessary to gain entry into social or business circles, and good deportment is considered the mark of an important person.

In Asia, propriety comes from the Confucian notion of honorable or correct behavior given the relationship and relative status of the parties. In some Asian countries, prescribed rules of conduct have been followed for hundreds, if not thousands, of years. Deviation from certain rules was considered a crime, at times provoking severe punishment, so the motivation to behave properly went well beyond the desire just to "be nice."

Rules of etiquette provide people with a sense of predictability. They act as a cushion against embarrassing surprises. It is possible that by ignoring local protocol you may cause your counterpart to lose face, and yourself to lose business in the process. By knowing the local social conventions, and being able to employ them or to blend in when desired, you ultimately have a greater effect on those you work with. This is the secret weapon of businesspeople with savoir faire.

Respect: The Antidote for Misunderstandings

In working with people anywhere, probably the most important aspect of your behavior is the display of respect. If it is apparent that you have respect for the other person and can show it, then minor faux pas are of little consequence. However, if it appears that you lack respect, then small infractions can be seen as major slights by the other party. The best way you can show respect to others is to learn their rules of etiquette and, in so doing, learn what displaying respect means to them.

Being an individualistic and egalitarian society, Americans often feel that no one deserves respect unless they earn it. Even then, some people are careful not to show too much deference. In many cultures, however, far from being demeaning, the act of showing respect elevates one's own respectability. We're not talking about being obsequious or groveling; we're talking about showing respect with dignity. This sort of respect motivates, and in some places obligates, the other party to behave in a respectful manner toward you.

When traveling abroad, it's usually wise to show respect to all, and deference to those whom others indicate are entitled to it. In some countries, being the buyer puts a person in the position of respect; in others, this status is not as important. People are naturally motivated to build relationships with people who show them respect. In cultures where business is driven by the relationship, it's all the more critical. You foster good relations by showing respect for those who expect it, whether you think they deserve it or not.

In America, as long as it's not openly disrespectful, not actively showing respect is a neutral behavior. In other countries, this "neutral" behavior can be interpreted as disrespect. In English, there is a distinction between the words *sir* and *mister.* The former is considered more polite, but not using "sir" would rarely be deemed an insult in America. In many cultures, such as the Japanese, there is almost a complete separate language of respect containing an honorific form of words when referring to the other party, and a humble form when referring to oneself. Many others have a more limited, but nevertheless distinctive, way of showing respect. Some cultures don't use the informal word for "you" until they are well-acquainted, such as *usted* (formal) versus *tu* (familiar) in Spanish and *sie* (formal) versus *du* (familiar) in German. To use the wrong form or level of speech in these cultures is considered offensive.

In the United States, respect is often granted for personal achievement, position, or salary. Unfortunately, gender and ethnic origin may also determine to whom we show respect. In many other countries, different criteria will be used. In Asia, India, Africa, and Latin America, age automatically commands respect. Additional factors could be the prestige of the company or organization and one's status or seniority within it. A person's connections at the company, or even outside the company, such as family or school ties, may be of extreme importance. Likewise, respect for you may be based on your connections to influential people, your title and position within your company, your savoir faire, and (sometimes the most difficult) the patience you exhibit. Since Americans value the self-made person, we are often embarrassed by any influential connections that may be viewed as part of our success. However, you may discover that it is more useful internationally to find a happy medium. You don't need to be a name-dropper, but at the same time you should realize that we don't work in isolation, and good connections do lend respectability. It is a way for people who don't know you to assess your credibility and trustworthiness.

Sometimes when Americans travel abroad, we inadvertently send the message that we are not worthy of respect. We do this in a number of ways. First, in America, humility is considered artificial rather than a real acknowledgment that nothing can be done alone. Accepting (and even demanding) credit when credit is due is a common American practice; patting yourself on the back for a job well done is considered healthy self-esteem. To many, however, this is viewed as egotistical arrogance, and certainly not the behavior of an honorable person. Thus we portray ourselves as not worthy of their respect. A second way Americans show they don't merit respect is through their propensity for informality and a tendency to equate formality with snobbery and coldness. However, what we consider friendly informality can be interpreted as lack of social refinement and disrespect for the other party. In some circles, our desire to be fair and evenhanded to all can go over like a lead balloon.

Americans feel uncomfortable reinforcing important status differences; they want to equalize everyone so the two sides can all be relaxed and informal and start telling jokes together. Here's a true story: An American delegation arrived in Taipei. The Taiwanese host firm picked up the delegates at Chiang Kai-shek Airport, putting the American CEO in a limousine with the Taiwanese CEO, and the rest of the American engineers and managers in a company van. During the ensuing days of sight-seeing and factory tours, the Americans—all being chummy equals on their first big trip to Asia —decided that each one of them should have their chance to ride in the limousine. So each day a different American rode with the Taiwanese CEO. Of course, the status-conscious Taiwanese CEO was deeply offended, concluding that the Americans were frivolous, disrespectful, and thus unaccountable—certainly not to be engaged with in business.

We also often fail to show respect to others on our delegation. Open competitiveness with coworkers or superiors may be the sign of an ambitious spirit in America, but to many it is the sign of an inferior character. Further, Americans can err by being overly impressed with personality, physical attractiveness, charisma, and personal achievement, all of which we equate with leadership. In many places, however, especially in Asia, the leader may be a quiet, self-effacing person. By devoting attention to someone with image rather then stature, we signal a lack of depth and, thus, accountability.

So, How Can We Show Respect?

Some ways of indirectly showing respect to foreign counterparts could include learning a little of their language, having a knowledge of their history, and being well versed in their customs. When dealing with individuals, you show respect for them by knowing how to pronounce their name (and their company's name) correctly; by knowing details of their past, such as their education; and by remembering details about them, such as their birthday and hobbies. These things take a little effort, but rarely cost you money, and their effect can have long-lived returns.

Hierarchical Egalitarian Status

There are many things in life that can contribute to one's status: wealth, power, blood line, achievements, physical stature, intelligence, and so on. How a culture deals with these inequalities is a reflection of how egalitarian or how hierarchically its people view relationships of all sorts. In the United States, even if we don't always treat people equally, the belief that we are equal in the eyes of the law is one that we hold dear. Our Declaration of Independence declares the concept that "all men are created equal" to be a self-evident truth. Although we believe there are differences in ability and circumstance, we bristle at the idea that someone is somehow innately "better" than others because of these. This view, however, is far from universal. Many cultures are hierarchical in nature, with clearly defined vertical, unequal relationships. Often these are reciprocal, complementary, and interdependent relationships: superiors may have unquestioned authority but at the same time are expected to be benevolent, paternalistic autocrats.

In hierarchical cultures, rules for social interaction between people of different status abound, and transgressions are little tolerated. Not only is the ritual of protocol fixed for interaction between people of different status, but also different behavior is expected of people within different levels of status. An obligation to observe higher degrees of protocol often comes with higher status. Lower-status people generally expect less decorum from each other.

In Asia, just getting introduced to people involves an interesting conflict in levels of heirarchy. This is why the business card (called a *meishi* in Japan and *mingpian* in China) is so critical. It provides all-important information about people's rank and status, and tells you how much deference you must show them. It's as if everyone had a rank insignia on their shoulder boards and knew his or her place in the commercial food chain. To rise in this type of hierarchy requires more than mere merit on the job; one's upward mobility and clout may have more to do with one's connections, one's family, one's age, the school one attended, or the mere size of one's company, rather than just one's competency on the job.

At the negotiation table, the Japanese, Chinese, or Korean side sits down in selected seats according to rank. At a banquet, they do the same. Inferiors bow and scrape in the presence of superiors. When an elder enters the room, look out; even the most brazen and Westernized Asian Generation X-er becomes the respectful mail clerk, greeting the elder with a traditional *salaam* in Indonesia, the *wai* in Thailand, or bowing repeatedly in Japan.

According to extensive studies conducted by Geert Hofstede, the most hierarchical countries are in Latin America, the Middle East, Africa, and Asia. Also high on the list, however, is France, followed by other southern European countries. More egalitarian than the United States are the northern European countries: Germany, Great

Britain, Switzerland, Scandinavia, Ireland, and Austria, as well as Israel and New Zealand. In hierarchical societies, you will generally find an autocratic management or teaching style, where employees expect to be given orders and their superiors are expected not to admit ignorance. You will also often find that with status comes extensive privilege and displays of deference.

In egalitarian societies, more equitable relationships are established between people of different status. Superiors are expected to consult and confer with their subordinates. Those with status or power should play down the appearance of it and should not be given special privileges. If you are working in a more egalitarian culture than you are used to, you may find that your position does not carry the automatic respect you are used to. Your ideas and opinions may be openly questioned, as may your orders if they seem out of line. Rules or consensus determine what is right, not the person in power.

Connected to the concept of hierarchy is the custom of formality. More egalitarian societies tend to be more informal in the way people communicate with each other, whereas hierarchical societies are inclined to formal codes of conduct and honorific forms of address. Formality reinforces hierarchy and power through the use of titles and ritualistic language. It reinforces lines of authority, and it also reduces chance, which can be considered dangerous. In Asia, where loss of face is a severe disgrace, the desire for predictability is great. Many of the overseas business environments in which you will do business are formal societies. It will be critical to your success that you honor this and not assume that by discounting formality you will either save time or make people more comfortable (e.g., trying to promote the use of first names). Informality can be interpreted as a sign of disrespect.

More formal cultures are not necessarily formal all the time, but they are formal more often and have a clearer distinction between which occasions are considered formal and which are considered informal. In the United States, although coworkers may loosen up over a happy-hour drink, there isn't a significant difference in the level of formality during this time and during work hours. In Japan, however, the difference is so extreme it may shock the uninitiated. Work time is much more formal than in this country, but in situations that are deemed "informal," they often outdo Americans in the way they let their hair down. The setting, the participants, and the occasion determine what is considered appropriate behavior and the degree of propriety expected.

Hierarchical societies require clear lines of authority; ceremony and formality are ways to enforce that clarity. What we see as freedom of self-expression, others may see as indulgent egocentric expression. The superior person shows restraint and doesn't "let it all hang out."

General Etiquette Lessons

Some of the general rules of etiquette around the world are not that different from ours. However, what we might consider somewhat impolite is often considered downright rude in other places—like blowing your nose in public, especially when eating; or putting your hands in your pocket while talking; or not exhibiting good posture. And failing to stand up when someone more important than you enters the room or sitting before invited to do so may be seen as a clear breach of etiquette.

Keep in mind that, in many places, you cannot partake of food or drink in public or in the presence of friends unless you are willing to share with others. For this reason, in much of the world it is considered rude to walk down the street eating something. Also, in the United States if people want to smoke, they will take out their pack of cigarettes, take one, and then put the pack away. Latin Americans would not do this; they *always* offer one to their companions before taking one for themselves.

In many areas of the world, guidelines for protocol have resulted from a desire for cleanliness. It is customary in Asia, the Middle

East, and much of Africa to remove your shoes before entering a home. For any who have adhered to this tradition, it is clear how much dirt is tracked into one's dwelling on shoes. Also in these areas, since the left hand is used to clean one's private parts, objects are given with the right hand only.

Be a Gracious Guest

When you are the guest, let your hosts take care of you. Don't deprive them of the opportunity to be gracious. Wait to be directed to your seat, for example. At a dinner, wait for the host to offer a toast or ask you to begin eating before you start. Even in a business setting, it's better to wait for the invitation. "When you enter a meeting in Indonesia," says Sam Black of IBM, "your hosts will likely ask if you would like some tea or coffee, but it won't be touched until you are invited to drink, often near the end of the meeting." In general, always *wait* to be invited to drink, to sit, to enter and leave a room, or to eat before partaking.

Nobody anywhere wants you to "ape" their mannerisms, or for you to try to become someone you are not. We don't like people from other countries who try to become too American either. First, they don't seem sincere; and second, it's easy to overdo something if you don't have enough experience or sensitivity. But when visitors don't follow certain conventions, they do appear rude.

Build Rapport. There are varying requirements for establishing rapport before business can be discussed, but almost everywhere else it's a stronger prerequisite for doing business than it is in the United States, so keep yourself apprised of topics people are likely to discuss. Read local newspapers. Listen while people are talking and try to perceive their interests. Look for things you have in common. Be aware of appropriate and inappropriate topics of conversation for that culture; bringing up sensitive political issues, for example, is a fast way to alienate your counterparts. Don't rush a meeting, and focus on trying to establish a true connection. Be prepared for the first meeting to be ceremonial. Remember that, especially in the implicit cultures, it will be necessary for them to establish a sense of trust. Don't ignore the need for a personal relationship, particularly in Asia, Africa, the Middle East, and South America.

Be on Your Best Behavior. It will always be up to you to decide when you are going to make a compromise or adaptation. When cultural compromise is not required, or possible, being well-mannered and polite, as defined in your own culture, is expected. Accentuate your formal behavior; it's almost always safer to err on the side of being too formal. Use last names with Mr. or Ms. and, in cultures where appropriate, use all the polite words your mother ever taught you. People don't expect you to know all their customs, but they do expect you to be what is considered polite and polished.

Make the Right First Impression. The last time you met someone, what made the first impression? What caught your attention? Chances are you noted the firmness of the handshake, the way the person was dressed, how friendly he or she seemed, and what his profession was or where she worked. The first impression makes a lasting one and may determine whether this is your last meeting or the beginning of a relationship. It's only natural that first impressions are based on cultural priorities, customs, and, yes, stereotypes. What this means, however, is that unconsciously you are likely to assume your counterpart is judging with the same criteria you use. This may be a serious mistake. Some of the components of a good first impression overseas include the following:

Appropriate dress. In choosing your overseas business attire, you should assume formality is expected unless you are certain it is otherwise (as it is in some very hot climes). Quality clothing is often respected as a sign of success and prosperity. Women should maintain the same level of formality in attire as men, although in India, where local women wear flowing colorful yards of cloth, a loose silk dress may blend in much better, as well as help you beat the heat. In much of the world, business dress is more conservative than in the United States and impeccable (down to the freshly shined shoes). Don't let your casual attitude toward dress give the impression that that is your attitude toward your host. Clothing standards are noticeably different between American and European business representatives. Middle-class Europeans are more conservative and more class-conscious than are Americans. The relaxed dress of some Americans is not seen in higher echelons of European business circles. It will quickly identify you as an American, and it can also incorrectly signal your lack of experience, professionalism, or seriousness about your effort. Conservative colors and fashions are the predominant features of the East European business dress code, too. At a trade show, virtually no one will be casually dressed or wearing an open-neck shirt, except perhaps at sporting-goods or recreational trade fairs.

Introducing yourself. Since connections count for a lot in much of the world, who is doing the introducing is the first critical issue. As much as possible, choose someone close to, and respected by, the party you are approaching. Usually, the more the stage has been set, and the more personal the introduction, the better. In other words, make sure that you supply the introducer with all pertinent information about yourself that might be useful. Says Mike Lorelli, "I worked for Apple Computer for a while. One of the most respected companies in France happens to be Apple Computer. I learned that if I am preintroduced, [if] someone is sending my bio to a government official in a foreign country, we make sure that Apple Computer is referenced in my background."

Business cards. The next item of importance will be the business card. Americans are often unprepared to even make a formal first impression using their business cards. First they have to find their business cards, looking through their pockets until they finally come across an old, worn-out card with the characteristic curve in it and hand it over with one hand instead of two, with the printing facing themselves rather than the receiver. Then they take the Asian's card (with one hand instead of two), failing to start formal, polite, and complimentary conversation based on the card, emphasizing the high status and rank of the other person. Finally, they put the Asian's card in a back pocket and *sit down on it.*

The business card carries more importance in many areas of the world than it does here, so make sure the printing and the stock it's printed on are of a quality that reflects the image you wish to project. Have plenty on hand and carry them in a card holder rather than in your wallet. When possible, have them printed in the local language in the manner that is customary there as well as in English on the other side. Put your logo on *their* side if you really want to impress them. Says Lorelli: "People really are flattered when they see that you respect their country. They never say it to you, but when you hand them a card, and it's in their language, you can see a little smile on their face."

In Asia, Africa, and the Middle East, be sure to give your card with your right hand. Be sure to read their cards thoroughly, especially in Asia; it contains important information on their status, and it is rude to simply put it aside without studying it. Marlene Rossman, an international maketing consultant, once received a card from a scruffy-looking Englishman and was surprised to see what she thought was a university acronym—until she realized that O.B.E. stood for Order of the British Empire!

Greeting rituals. The initial greeting usually consists of both an action and certain customary words. These, however, differ greatly throughout the world. Although most people with even minimal international awareness will probably expect you to shake hands, it may behoove you to start paying attention to the local custom and following it when you feel comfortable. In Japan people bow to each other; in India they put their palms together in a *namaste* to honor the Godhead in the other person; Malays will "greet you from the heart" by putting their right hand to their chest; Thais bow and put their hands together similar to a *namaste,* but only the fingertips touch and they are spread apart. Many Africans will clap their hands as they bow. Many Europeans and Arab men will kiss both cheeks when they greet friends. For the most part, business-people everywhere greet Westerners by shaking hands, though what is considered a proper handshake differs greatly. As Arabs shake hands, they may put their left hand on the other's shoulder. Mexicans have gentle and lingering handshakes, French light and short. Japanese handshakes are even softer, and are often performed while bowing. In Europe, as well as many other protocol-conscious areas, expect to shake hands both at the beginning and end of meetings. Mexicans, additionally, have the *abrazo,* which is like a friendly bear hug.

Spoken greetings in foreign countries are often loaded with more meaning than the perfunctory "how do you do?" The Hebrew *shalom* or Arabic *salam* means "peace." Some desert Arabs take this further, wishing the other a day of jasmine and cream, both of which are scarcities. The Japanese announce that it is the first time they are meeting and ask the other to look upon the relationship in a favorable way. The French are "enchanted" and the south Germans "greet God." Since these greetings carry a special meaning, it's nice to be able to say them correctly in the local language.

Getting names and titles right. Remember the importance of rank and respect. Various cultures routinely call people by their titles, such as president, manager, or minister. Where this is customary, to not do it is an obvious irregularity. In Mexico, any educated person, including most middle managers, have degrees reflected in the common title "Licenciado," a term with some prestige. It is therefore unflattering to call your counterpart Señor Salinas, instead of Licenciado Salinas, if that is his title.

Some cultures respect educational degrees more than others and will grant you differing levels of respect depending on your expertise area. In the United Kingdom, for example, engineers are so plentiful that many are on the dole; noting your engineering background on your business card won't win you points there. In France and Germany, however, having a background in engineering elicits the same reaction as in America when you say you went to Harvard or were a Rhodes Scholar.

In Asia, titles don't just indicate a person's position, but for many it's a tribute to their group identity as well. President, director, manager, and section chief are common company titles indicating status within the group. Many Asians will call children "older brother" or "older sister," and familiar adults senior to them "aunt" or "uncle." In other words, it's not just a reflection of rank, but a reflection of belonging.

Titles are used to substitute for a person's first name. The Germans, for instance, always use "Herr" and "Fräulein" before a person's title or last name, even when speaking in English. German executives call their secretaries by the title "Fräulein" only. If you socialize with a German over time, you will eventually be prompted to link right arms, with drinks in hand, and toast "Brüderschaft," or brotherhood. Only then should you consider yourself on a first-name basis.

Personal names pose the biggest problems in Asia and Latin America. In Asia the family name comes first. Thus Tanaka (family name) Kenji (given name) is Mr. Tanaka. In China, Liu Wei-da is Mr. Liu. What makes the situation most confusing is that when writing in English, many, but by no means most, reverse this custom for our benefit. If you are not sure, ask. Thais, on the other hand, place their given name first like in the West, but commonly use these instead of the unwieldy last. Thus, Vanchai (given name) Mahatanankoon (family name) becomes Mr. Vanchai, or Manager Vanchai. Confusing the situation further is that Chinese and Korean women don't take their husband's name.

In Latin America a person's father's family name is followed by the person's mother's family name. Carlos Fernandez Salas would be called Mr. Fernandez, Salas being his mother's family. His wife is Blanca Garcia de Fernandez and is called Mrs. Fernandez. Their son's name is Jaime Fernandez Garcia. And just to make it more difficult, in Brazil the two names may be reversed.

Customs of touching and interpersonal distance. What is considered appropriate "touching" varies greatly around the world. In many places it is not uncommon for members of the same gender to walk down the street holding hands, German women, for example, and Arab men. When Yasser Arafat made his first tour of a police base in Gaza City with Brigadier General Youssef Nasser of the Palestinian police after the historic agreement with Israel, it was truly a Kodak moment for cross-cultural protocol specialists. Throughout the momentous inspection, the two walked along holding hands.

Touching the wrong person at the wrong time, however, or in the wrong place, can be highly offensive. In Asia, in general, there is not much interpersonal touching (even shaking hands is not a tradition), so patting a colleague on the back is not a welcome gesture. As the evening progresses, however, the rules are less rigid, and after enough alcohol they often go out the window. South America is another matter. People frequently touch one another as a warm and friendly gesture. In John Graham's studies, the Brazilians were the only negotiators who touched one another during meetings, with the seller often leaning across the table to touch the buyer's arm. In Thailand, a person's head is considered sacred, so it is imperative that you never touch a Thai's head, or even pass an object over it.

Appropriate interpersonal distance, or proximity, also differs throughout the world. It will always depend on the relationship of the parties—much more distance is assigned to strangers than to friends and family. Generally, Middle Easterners, southern Europeans, and Latin Americans prefer a closer span: too much separation appears cool and standoffish. So backing up when a counterpart is trying to communicate a sense of warm companionship can throw cold water on the business. Others, such as Asians (in formal situations) and some northern Europeans, prefer more interpersonal distance than Americans. By taking a step closer to get within the "friendly" range (for us), we can actually drive them away by "invading their space."

Knowing who's who. If you are unclear of the rank of your counterparts, watch who walks into the room first, who is introduced first, and who exits an elevator first. Since modesty is a virtue in Asia, important people may be self-effacing. Watch who defers to whom.

When and where to be punctual. What is considered early, on time, "fashionably late," and undesirably late also varies from country to country. The more linear a people, the more concerned they tend to be with punctuality. Prior appointments and punctual arrivals are a necessity in northern Europe and Asia. In fact, many northern Europeans view tardiness as a sign of an undisciplined person, never mind that 8:00 A.M. is a common time for business appointments in Germany. People tend to be more casual about punctuality in southern Europe and Latin America. But even there, it depends on your position and relationship to the other party. In Spain, for example, there are very specific, unwritten rules about who can be late, and by how long, both in professional and social situations. In Madrid, it is not in your best interest to arrive at a business meeting (or a job interview) prior to the agreed time, as this will give the impression that you are overeager. Instead, it is better to arrive either just on time or one to five minutes late. On the other hand, the person from whom you want something (e.g., a contract) may make you wait for some time before seeing you. "The reasons for this can be multiple," says an American working in Spain, "from having scheduled too many things at once to having unexpected emergencies come up, but that same privilege is not well looked upon when you are the soliciting party."

Body language. In addition to offensive gestures, it is important to be aware of inadvertant body language that sends the wrong message. In Asia and the Middle East, it is extremely rude to expose the bottom of your foot or shoe, especially pointing it at someone. Putting your feet on tables or chairs is also taboo in much of the world. As mentioned earlier, posture is very important too. In Asia and much of Europe, people stand and sit up very straight. If they cross their legs, it's a tight cross, or at the ankles. Americans often stand with their hands in their pockets, leaning forward. In Mexico this is seen as an aggressive stance. Yet Mexicans commonly stand with their arms crossed while in business or casual discussions.

Dining Etiquette

Eating utensils and the way we use them differ around the world. The Continental style is to use the fork in the left hand and knife in the right hand throughout the meal. Laotians use a fork in the left hand and a spoon in the right. In traditional Japanese and Chinese restaurants, chopsticks will be provided and forks may or may not be available, so if you haven't yet mastered the art of the sticks, now is a good time to start learning. In India, the Middle East, and Africa, traditional meals are eaten with the hands—the right hand, that is—except to break the bread, when both hands are used. Internationally accepted manners dictate that one should keep one's hands visible during the meal (don't put one on your lap while you eat) but not with elbows on the table.

Subtle differences between American and Continental table manners can cause trouble. The writer and editor Ken Jacobson accompanied one of his editors on a visit to Paris. They were lunching in the corporate dining room of a major French corporation. The editor, says Ken, "was eating and left his fork and knife on opposite sides of his plate, but crossed at the edge of the plate away from him in an inverted V shape." In France, this means you intend to continue eating. If you have finished eating, you put your knife and fork parallel and diagonal across the plate nearer the middle, from the right of the plate near you slanting toward the left away from you. "I knew that my editor had finished," says Ken, "but the waiter didn't—he just assumed that he was going to continue, because that was the sign he was reading in the plate." The waiter grew more and more nervous. "He realized that my editor had finished, but in France you don't ask."

If you are queasy about what you eat (sheep's eye, fish eye, rodent, dog, camel, snake, or gorilla) either let your hosts know ahead of time or don't ask. Because once it's offered, saying "no thank you" is impolite. Mike Lorelli concurs:

> I had an amusing dining experience in Oslo as an international representative of Playtex. I traveled to Oslo, Norway, realizing it was a town of fishermen; you eat fish at breakfast, lunch, and dinner. So I was prepared. When in Rome, do as the Romans do, right? With a Norwegian general manager, I ate raw fish for breakfast. You can't put it aside and ask for your bagel and cream cheese; you have to eat his raw fish. The last thing you want to do is offend them. Then, later in the day raw fish was served for lunch . . . and that night, raw fish again for dinner. I have to tell you that by that time I was almost gagging. Then the waiter came over to our table and tried to offer some dessert. In broken English he said, "Oh you have to try our specialty dessert . . . we have cake with whale nuts." I was saying to myself, "Oh, God . . . I am really earning my salary today." But there was no way that I was going to offend this general manager in his homeland and I ordered the cake with the whale nuts. When the waiter brought it over it turned out that it was cake with *walnuts*. Thank God.

Tipping is unusual in Japan, China, Iceland, and Tahiti. But in other places, a gratuity of 10 to 20 percent of the dinner bill will be expected if it is not already included. It's wise to tip (To Insure Promptness) all who assist you in Latin America and the Middle East, except for taxi drivers. If your research hasn't covered this nicety, consult the concierge at your hotel or a colleague on what is customary.

Business Entertaining

Whether in Taipei, Warsaw, São Paulo, or elsewhere, it's not just male bonding and trust building that takes place during drinking sessions and afternoon rounds of golf. A truly awesome amount of real business dealing is being done in these settings. Fortune 500 companies which sell one-of-a-kind technology can afford to go into Asia playing by seller's rules—no gifts, no bar hopping, no payoffs, no singing at the *karaoke* bar. But for the majority of companies selling to Asia, part of their competitive advantage is how well they perform in the floating world of business schmoozing.

Libations. You have to enter overseas markets with your own personal code of business ethics firmly set and clear in your mind. And it must be a code not alterable by large quantities of alcohol. And God forbid that your code of ethics completely prohibits the imbibing of alcohol. Whether sipping *soju* in Seoul, *maotai* in Manchuria, aged tequila in Mexico, or *sake* in Osaka, you lose the chance to get closer to your friends (unless they are Muslims) by refusing liquor, unless you are armed with a believable excuse like you have a truly life-threatening stomach ulcer or it is against your religion. That's the only way you're going to get out of *stolich* or *gambei,* or whatever the local bottoms-up toast might be.

In much of the world, socializing is a part of business, so by all means go when invited. Although alcohol is outlawed in some countries and religions, in many cultures it's close to the cornerstone of "bonding" in a business relationship. From Moscow to Tokyo, and from *maotai* to scotch, many deals have been cemented as a result of the camaraderie people feel from loosening up together. The trick, however, is to build a bond without getting drunk, even if you have to fake it a little in the process. When you're negotiating, drinking too much is a definite liability: You may say things you didn't intend to say or the other side may have a tag team to take over the negotiations from your counterpart the next day. The trouble is, with alcohol you're not used to, it can sneak up on you, so pace yourself—your contract may rely on it.

Entertaining in Asia is usually outside of the home, but elsewhere you may well be invited to someone's home. The type of entertainment can range from the Japanese *karaoke* singing bars to a feast at someone's house. Says Sam Black, IBM representative in Indonesia: "Business socializing in Indonesia is constant. You block off four evenings a week on your calendar for going to some kind of a function; one of those four will be a party held at someone's home. A lot of business gets done in these social environments, a lot of schmoozing and talking and discussion. It's a system that works."

Toasting will often be a huge part of a banquet, particularly in parts of Asia and the former Soviet republics. In Georgia, the host is the toastmaster for the ritual. He is called a *tamada*. He will toast everything: you, your wife, your company, your venture, peace, the kitchen help—everything. Whether the toast is with vodka or wine, you have to toss it all back. Don't leave a drop, or you will be compromising the toast. In order to make a toast yourself, ask the toastmaster before doing so; the *tamada* will usually permit it. If toasting is to last throughout the evening, we recommend that you try to toast alternately with members of both your team and theirs; that your team toast in descending order of team rank; and that, at the end of the festivities, your number-one person offer the last toast, at which time you should thank the host and toast his or her good health.

What if you are a nondrinker? Olga Ringo, a consultant and CIS travel specialist in San Francisco, says, "The Russians *drink*. And you have to be able to be one of the fellows who can handle that. I don't drink, so I tell them I have an ulcer." Also, she holds her glass up and sips, without gulping down the contents during a toast, preventing her glass from being constantly refilled. The Russian side won't necessarily drain their glass during a toast, but they may expect you to. So again, claim you have a medical condition. "Doctor's orders." If possible, it behooves you to refrain from imbibing while socializing with Muslims. Says Sam Black, "There's a lot of drinking in Indonesia—of 7-Up, of orange drink—but when they pass the tray, it's usually nonalcoholic, though beer is common and hard drinks uncommon. Foreigners can drink alcohol without offending."

The Ritual of Gift Giving

In the United States, we give gifts rather lightly—for Christmas, Hanukkah, birthdays, and so on. In many other cultures, however, gift giving is serious business. The gifts you give and receive, depending on the culture, can gain you respect, further business relationships, bring favors, and ensure your success.

Mike Lorelli:

> For this Japan trip on which I was to meet our joint venture partner—the CEO of the joint venture—I had all my ducks in a row, or so I thought. I had my Japanese cards, worked on my bows, I had studied up on his background, and had refreshed myself on Japanese business culture, geography, history so I'd be reasonably conversant . . . and the one thing I completely forgot was the gift. So I'm having breakfast with my local guy in the hotel before we are to go to this guy's office and it hits me like a ton of bricks: I forgot the gift. The ultimate faux pas. And of course, if you are giving a gift to a senior Japanese official, an American item has a heck of a lot more value than if you give them something that's not recognizable from any particular geography. At the time I was sitting at this breakfast, I had on a set of Pepsico cuff links, which are only given to presidents of Pepsico divisions. It doesn't say Pepsico, but they

had the red, white, and blue swirl logo, on a gold circle. You would only recognize them if you were working for Pepsi or if you knew somebody who worked for Pepsi. Otherwise you wouldn't make the connection. So I rushed to a department store across the street and bought a pair of cuff links, just to get the box. I put those cuff links on, and took mine off and put them in the box, wrapped them up, and gave them to this guy. When I gave them to him I said, "I want you to know that these cuff links are only given to presidents of Pepsico's divisions, and I want you to have a pair." Now this guy was absolutely taken, bowled over. He took us out to dinner later that night and you bet he had those damn things on, and he was lookin' at them every five minutes; they were his new prize possession in life.

Every globalizing company needs a gift-giving policy. A question that should be addressed is: When your firm's representatives give gifts, what are they trying to accomplish—show appreciation, build a stronger friendship, generate obligation, or obtain a signature? Most of the Fortune 500 firms we interviewed reported that they don't give gifts of high value; it seemed that the smaller the firm, the more gifts play a role in the maintenance of business relationships. One thing we heard often was that no firm wanted to do business with a partner who *had* to be given gifts as a matter of course, echoing the words of the eighteenth-century British wit and scholar Thomas Fuller, who said: "A friend that you buy with presents will be bought from you."

Many U.S. companies—especially Fortune 500 companies—have put in place no-gift-giving or gift-receiving policies. For instance, IBM is not a gift-giving or -receiving company. IBM's representative in Jakarta sends back all gifts "with a nice note explaining that it is the policy of IBM to treasure [our distributors] for the quality of their service, and that IBM would not want it construed that it selected the distributor on the basis of any other sort of decision process." Of course, the Indonesians can't believe that IBM won't accept their gifts, because the practice is so ingrained there and free of ethical considerations. It's like inviting a friend to Christmas morning or Chinese New Year. You have wrapped gifts for your guest and your children, but he won't accept them as a matter of principle. How are you going to feel having your gifts rejected? If he accepts, how is he going to feel if he's not allowed to give anything in return?

A no-gift-giving code can absolve representatives from becoming obligated to generous foreign parties; in this case, you will want to instruct your representatives how to gracefully refuse a gift both verbally and in writing. Instruct them not to embarrass the foreign team by overtly rejecting gifts; have them accept the gift and thereby validate the giver's intention without suffering a loss of face. In one case, a team of negotiators from a company were given $5,000 Rolex watches by their Japanese counterparts. Luckily, their intermediary told the Americans to accept the gifts when they were presented, and then later the company sent them back. When gifts are returned, have representatives state how much the company appreciates the gifts but that company policy prevents them from accepting them. There are always cases where you cannot gracefully decline a gift. Pomeranz advises: "If we have to accept a gift, we try to do so with very good grace. The gifts become company property, they're donated for charity, or used for employee incentive awards. We don't keep them."

We recommend that you consider playing the "gift game," and give gifts to business partners, their children, and anyone who helps you do anything. An old Chinese proverb reminds us: "The man with buttoned pockets, no one will do him a favor." What you give and when will differ from culture to culture, so do your homework! Like any other game, the more you know the nuances, the better you will be at playing. The gifts you give should reflect the kind of relationship you desire. Giving a book on the redwoods to a Japanese delegation can be an example of the solidity of your partnership, or you might consider technical books to your counterpart at the Academy of Science. Never give a letter opener or a knife set, because they can symbolize a severing of the relationship in many cultures. Former President Reagan once gave Mexico's president an antique rifle; considering our two histories, that probably didn't sit too well with Mexicans.

Asians tend to give gifts more often than Westerners. They wish to cement interdependent relationships. From presents to supplying information to doing a favor, these gifts repay indebtedness or ensure that the receiver can be counted on in the future. When debts are outstanding, there is an obligation that the other party may "cash in" when needed. To avoid this, Asians are always trying to make sure they are on the "accounts receivable" end, as should you. Probably most obsessive about this practice are the Japanese. One study showed that a typical Japanese family gave or received about 30 gifts (ranging from trinkets to presents and favors) per month! Needless to say, you do not want to get caught up in the custom at this level; however, a certain degree of involvement will be seen as a sign of good will.

Gifts from your home country are the best: a coffee-table picture book, a gold quality pen, chocolate, wine, bourbon, an item specific to your locale, a high-quality logo gift (not made in the country you are visiting), or something from a famous place. When giving to a group, try to choose something everyone can enjoy. When giving to an individual, do it in private and try to make it something personal. Pick up on cues about the person's interest. Does he like high-tech things? Does she like music? How about a compact disc? Does he collect stamps, coins, T-shirts, or gadgets? If you can, mention the conversation that made you think the person would like that item when you present it.

Always wrap gifts nicely, but, in Japan, don't unwrap one you've received in their presence unless they ask you to; then do it carefully. Thank the person at the time and then again the next time you speak or write to the person. Again, avoid giving scissors, knives, letter openers, or four (a homonym for death) of anything. And don't write an Asian's name in red ink.

Europeans and Latin Americans tend to give gifts more in a social or business atmosphere, to thank someone for an invitation or a favor, and not at the outset of a business relationship. Try to be tasteful in your choice, neither cheap nor extravagant. Remember that in Christian countries 13 is considered unlucky, and in French-speaking cultures chrysanthemums are for funerals. Generally, you don't give a gift to your host when you arrive, but wait until toward the end of your visit, except when invited to a person's house.

Always alert your host that you are going to give a gift if it's significant. For example, tell him that you will be bringing a gift to his office before leaving for the airport. That way, if you are giving to a group, the whole group will be present. Give individual gifts only in private; and give to a group during a scheduled group gathering when everyone is present. The worst mistake you can make in East Europe is to rob someone of face by giving gifts to their colleagues and forgetting them. As strange as it may sound, a terrific gift is the conference proceedings to an important round-table or seminar program. Information is scarce in Eastern Europe; important, recently published research brings much prestige to scholars and scientists. But in East Europe, business gift-giving should be kept to a minimum. As a way to forge bonds of friend-ship, it's okay, but as a manipulative tool, no. If someone is only motivated by you giving them gifts, you're dealing with the wrong person. Bring gifts from the West, but don't worry about bringing expensive gifts.

In Islamic countries, alcohol is out of the question as a gift. Books, cassette tapes, pens, or calculators make good gifts. Go out of your way to avoid making it look like a bribe, such as giving it in public or only after a personal relationship has been established. You may take a present for his children, but not for his wife.

Be a Gracious Host

Throughout the world, people pride themselves on their hospitality. Arabs are obligated by religion and custom to share whatever they have with a guest, even a stranger. This may be a hardship to the host, but they take great pride and joy in the tradition. In Latin America, the mere act of suggesting makes you the host. A Mexican national working for an American company in Mexico complained that on Fridays, some of the Americans would say, "Let's go out to the cantina and have some drinks." When it was time to pay, however, the Americans would announce that the outing was "Dutch." The Mexicans would be shocked because in Mexico, if you invite someone out, it is assumed you will pay.

Business hosting on the part of your company should be taken very seriously. In America we tend to have a "help yourself" style of hosting because Americans like to be self-sufficient. But in other countries they have the "be my guest" attitude. In other words, your guests are unlikely to reach across the table to take the cream and sugar because they are waiting for you to offer it to them. If you are hosting a dinner, either be aware of their seating traditions or explain why someone is being seated where they are, such as "we put the guest at the head of the table" or "this has the best view." In a social setting, you may want to place people of the same rank from each team together, so that they can become better acquainted.

The first rule to follow is to remember that business counterparts visiting your country may not plan things themselves because they are expecting that you, as the host, will be scheduling their time. Even at a business meeting, you will be responsible for deciding where each person sits (in few places is the helter-skelter American-style seating acceptable), what refreshments are served and when, as well as the agenda. In performing introductions and indicating where each person will sit, don't forget the need for formality and hierarchy. At a meeting you may want to seat teams with counter-parts of equal rank sitting opposite them. Opening and closing statements will be expected. And when the meeting is over, it is highly advisable to see your guests to the elevator, door, or taxi. Wait until they're out of sight, lest they look back to wave good-bye one last time.

Be aware of your guests' dietary customs. Jews who keep kosher do not eat pork or shellfish or mix dairy and meat products in the same meal. Muslims do not eat pork or drink alcohol. Many Hindus and Buddhists are vegetarians. Also keep in mind that giving guests a tour of your house could be interpreted by many as showing off, since this is not done in much of the world.

Part I: Assessing Yourself for Protocol Power

Answer each item by circling the appropriate number on the continuum below:

To Almost No Extent			To Some Extent		To a Great Extent			To a Very Great Extent	
1	2	3	4	5	6	7	8	9	10

Before arriving in another country, I make sure that I know at least the basic rules of business etiquette there, including how to greet and address people.

1   2   3   4   5   6   7   8   9   10

I keep in mind that in some countries, to know and emphasize ceremony in business dealings is a way to show respect for the people I am doing business with.

1   2   3   4   5   6   7   8   9   10

I insist that my colleagues who accompany me overseas know the basic rules of social etiquette in the country we are visiting.

1   2   3   4   5   6   7   8   9   10

I understand that in some countries I will be treated differently from others because of my status compared to theirs, and that I should treat others with their status and rank in mind as well.

1   2   3   4   5   6   7   8   9   10

I know how to generate conversation with acquaintances in other countries *while* remaining formal and polite.

1   2   3   4   5   6   7   8   9   10

Part II: Assessing Your Company for Protocol Power

My firm has provided training to its international staff in general social etiquette and business diplomacy.

1   2   3   4   5   6   7   8   9   10

My firm ensures that its traveling staff members understand the rules of protocol in a country before sending them there on business.

1   2   3   4   5   6   7   8   9   10

My firm instructs its international staff about how to sustain rapport with foreign business acquaintances while avoiding certain sensitive topics that can be insulting.

1   2   3   4   5   6   7   8   9   10

My company checks with cultural experts about the appropriateness of gifts before giving them to foreign guests.

1   2   3   4   5   6   7   8   9   10

My firm makes a special effort to properly host international guests, from handling their transportation to entertaining them with sight-seeing and banquets.

1   2   3   4   5   6   7   8   9   10

As before, add up your score for each section of this quiz. If you or your firm scores 25 or lower out of a possible total of 50, the area of protocol power should be a key priority for you and your company.

Helping Your Firm Globalize

You probably feel yourself growing more aware of, and comfortable with, the essential components of global excellence. But you may also have realized (possibly the hard way) that it's one thing to upgrade one's skills and attain international expertise, but quite another for the entire staff of a company to acquire such skills. Since more than one level of a typical multinational engages with more than one level of a foreign firm, the need for companywide global skill building has reached a crescendo. The challenge that globalism entails for CEOs, managers, and workers is to generate top-to-bottom commitment to international excellence.

In a cautionary tale of good intentions and prudent preparation gone to waste, Frank Burham confronted the monster face-to-face. In the late 1960s, Burham became president of an electronic components manufacturer in San Diego called Mepco, which was owned by the giant Dutch conglomerate Philips Electronics. Before it was purchased by Philips in 1969, Mepco had granted a license to a Japanese company called Copal to use its production technology for printing the inks on ceramic substrates and gluing the circuitry to the ceramic.

Copal used Mepco's technology in manufacturing components inside high-volume consumer products like VCRs and cassette players, which were pouring out of Japan in the 1970s and 1980s. Meanwhile, Mepco was using the same technology to produce components mainly for the defense industry in the United States. As volume grew, Mepco moved its production facility to Mexico, where it could benefit from that country's cheap labor. By the mid-1970s, Mepco employed 300 people in its Mexico-based *maqui-*

ladora and 150 people in a San Diego facility. As time went on, however, Mepco found that it could not compete with Copal and other Japanese suppliers of the same product because the Japanese simply produced a higher quality product. By 1986, Mepco was essentially doomed.

"So by the classic argument that if you can't beat them, join them," says Burham, "we joined the Japanese." Mepco solicited Copal to become its partner and Copal agreed. The deal was signed and the new company, called Mepcopal, became 50-percent owned by Copal of Japan and 50-percent owned by Philips Electronics of Holland. Burham would spend the next decade caught between two very different international corporate cultures.

As Copal prepared to bring in their manufacturing equipment and install it in San Diego, Burham set about preparing as best he could for managing the interface between the two partners. "We looked for a way to develop some knowledge of working with the Japanese," he says. "We knew we were going to be constantly involved with them, and they were going to be coming over here often."

Burham brought in one of the authors (Rowland) to conduct Japanese culture and language training sessions with groups of people at the company for a period of three months, a couple of afternoons a week. "We all realized that none of us was ever going to speak Japanese very well, but that wasn't our objective. It was more just to put forth the effort so we could have at least some interchange and dialogue, and not just be totally cold toward them." It is rare to find companies willing to invest in preventive training as Burham did; most firms initiate training as a crisis management move after serious problems with a foreign partner have already materialized.

The result of early preparation? "It really helped us a lot," Burham says. "When the Japanese engineers and managers began to arrive to set up the equipment and train us, they found that we had all of this Japanese training, and so everything went very smoothly. I think that the Japanese were surprised that we had put in that much effort before they even got here."

Burham's superior (we'll call him Jones) was a corporate officer for Philips Electronics. Headquarters sent him in to sign contracts and other documents with the Japanese partner and to generally monitor the situation. Unfortunately, says Burham, "Jones was very, very anti-Japanese and very 'ugly-American' in his approach. I tried to expose him to some of the Japan training material, and I tried to talk to him about [the cultural issues]. But he put himself above that. His thinking was: If they want to do business with us, they're going to do it on my terms."

Jones was a cross-cultural Chernobyl. During the first meeting with the Japanese, when the two teams were getting introduced, one of the Americans addressed a Japanese member in Japanese. Jones burst out: "This is an American deal! We won't be speaking any Japanese here!" Burham remembers how he personally was driven by the fact that if Mepco did not affiliate with the Japanese, the company was doomed. "We needed them." But the approach of Jones from Philips was: We're big Philips and *they need us.*

During meetings, Jones was not aware, says Burham, that the Japanese never say no. "They will sit there and listen to you and nod their heads and respond 'yes' to acknowledge that they understand what you are saying. He would take 'yes' for an answer and steam ahead until it was a one-sided dialogue; he'd walk away from the meeting figuring that everything was all set. He couldn't comprehend why nothing was happening. After all, he'd had a good meeting and he'd given his speech and they all said 'yes' and they all were smiling and parted friends. But that was it." Jones became livid that the Japanese weren't responding; there was never any outward confrontation on their part, but they just weren't responding.

Although most of the Japanese who negotiated on behalf of Copal could read English well, they would not speak English because they didn't feel confident doing so. So they had hired an interpreter. Jones, however, was taken aback during the evening banquet when many of the Japanese negotiators began talking to him in English. The Japanese had to get into that environment and be loosened up before they would speak in English. Moreover, says Burham, "there were normally two or three of us and ten or twelve of them at each business meeting, as well as five or six other onlookers at each meeting. I knew what was going on but my boss from Philips didn't know what was happening." Tensions mounted, and Burham worked behind the scene through his Japanese counterpart, who was very Westernized. "He was my go-between. He had excellent English skills and had lived in the United States for ten years or so. He was my primary interface and I could talk to him about this cultural stuff and he would go back and calm his people down."

In addition to producing for the U.S. market, the new partnership was also to export product back to Japan. The concept was that over a period of time, sales to Japan would decrease and U.S. consumption would rise. That was the theory. "In practice," says Burham, "it took the Philips sales organization much longer to develop domestic volume." The sales goals that Philips committed to were never met. The reason, he says, was that "Philips was not aggressive in marketing the product." As the years dragged on, the Japanese became fretful. They had agreed to take back production for only two years, and now it had been eight years.

Burham saw the writing on the wall: He had to either help the Japanese partner force Philips to sell the product better or the venture was going to fail. He started by asking Philips executives directly at annual meetings about their efforts to market the product. Moreover, he urged the Japanese partners to demand that Philips make concrete commitments to push the product harder, and to question Philips's contracted "best efforts."

"Make them sell," Burham told the Japanese. "Make them sell; they're not doing their job." But, he says, "that was far too confrontational for them. They really couldn't bring themselves to tell somebody that they were doing a bad job. In my personal discussions with them, they expressed their disappointment; they knew what was going on. But they didn't want to tell their partner that it was doing a bad job. They decided to see whether things would improve by just waiting. I was not able to get them to take a forceful position."

Finally, the Japanese came to the conclusion that the deal was not working. The joint venture partnership would have to be dissolved. "The Japanese became very disappointed and the people who were originally involved in the venture were blamed," says Burham. "Everyone at Copal involved in this thing has been pushed completely out of the organization, with the exception of the director, who has finally regained his position as director of international marketing after four years. And if he hadn't been fluent in English and Chinese and some German, he probably would have been purged with all the rest of them. Anybody who was associated with this venture was considered to have created an embarrassing situation."

The Japanese did not take the steps necessary along the way to prevent the end result of failure and embarrassment. "I didn't anticipate that they would roll over and die that easily," Burham says. "It was very important to them to be involved with a very large, high-prestige, and high-visibility company." Philips was one of the largest manufacturers in the world, and the Japanese were delighted to be affiliated with this world-renowned giant.

"I think they were so captivated by that, that they couldn't conceive that Philips could do anything wrong."

End result: In late 1993 the equipment was packed up and shipped back to Japan. Copal would continue to supply the product to the U.S. side on an export basis, with Mepco acting merely as an importer.

Frank Burham learned the hard way that while you must be personally committed to international excellence, so must your company. You need international skills at both personal and corporate levels. But who is going to take responsibility for instilling international excellence among your coworkers, middle managers, and up on "the fourteenth floor"? (This was the phrase John Delorean used to refer to insularized upper management during his years as a vice president at General Motors.)

A firm may need to organize differently for global business, train its people differently, and set up unique systems for bringing its affiliates closer together, while also giving them room to nimbly seek out opportunities and manage them. The firm may need to carry out wrenching changes in its hierarchies. Teams of people from different countries may need to work together toward a common objective, with the effort being delicately coordinated from above with culturally astute kid gloves. It's not going to be easy, and it's too early to just imitate success stories, even if tangible "formulas" were easily transferrable to your firm. It's going to take *commitment*—the final strategy of the international excellence paradigm—both on your part and that of your company.

What went wrong with this cross-border venture? A plethora of weaknesses and missteps ensured failure. First, there was a lack of cross talk. Mepco was not networked with its owner, Philips, in such a way that upper corporate management could be moved to constructive action. Communication links were not kept open and clear. Second, Mepco could not take advantage of Philips's size. Marketing brochures used by Philips, for example, carried the Mepcopal brand name and did not feature Philips Electronics. Mepco was never brought into the Philips family of companies. The parent issued no pan-Philips philosophy or values, nor did it generate enthusiasm or team synergy between parent and sibling. Third, leadership of the team sent to Japan was turned over to a corporate "suit" with no connection to the participating unit. Any team spirit already forged by Frank Burham was lost. The entire venture would have run smoother without any direct participation of Philips or its high-level representative at all. Fourth, Jones was inept and shouldn't have been placed in an international position in the first place, at least not without proper training, preferably along with the Mepco team.

At the very root of all of Mepcopal's problems was one ineluctable fact: while Mepco enjoyed limited autonomy, it received no real support from the parent. Philips wanted control but it did not want to take the responsibility to make the deal work. Many business schools, in fact, now use Philips as a case study of how a company can really do things wrong internationally. In the early 1990s, the company was losing so much money that its stockholders got together and forced a management change; many of the firm's European managers were part of the old Philips family. A new CEO was brought in to restructure, which entailed massive layoffs and wild pruning of Philips's businesses. A joke circulated in the world financial community that if you see a building with the Philips name on it, it's for sale.

You need to ask whether your firm is internationally dysfunctional like Philips was, or whether it has its global act together. You may feel that you don't have much control over your company's global direction, that you are out of the loop in generating globalism. But companies are made up of people. You *can* do a number of things to assist your company, depending on your position.

First, we urge you to take some notes on the following questions. As a manager, you can collect feedback on these issues from your staff, on a confidential basis. You may be able to convince your boss to submit the best ideas to the CEO for use in creating a company action plan for going international.

• What steps does my company need to take in order to become a global company, especially in its corporate policies?

• What might the company change in the way it operates domestically that will benefit the way it operates globally; for example, in stretching out its perspective to be longer term?

• Is upper management committed to globalizing the firm and its people? Companies don't work by directive; they work by example. Unless upper management is committed to international excellence, it's not going to happen.

• What are some things that my department needs to do to be more international? What changes in my work group should I work toward to make it more international?

• Perhaps most important, what *obstacles* exist in the way of taking these steps (e.g., budget constraints, lack of support from upper management, resistance from the parent company)?

This last question should be considered carefully. Perhaps the ideas you have in mind will cause others to worry about their jobs, or fear more work. Perhaps the CEO is not a listener but a dictator. You might recall the story about how Japanese automobile companies set up their assembly lines so that any worker on the line could pull a lever to stop the line if he or she noticed a quality problem. Later, U.S. automobile companies set up similar levers on some of their assembly lines. Well, global excellence needs to be put in everybody's hands too. Does a lever exist at your firm so that anyone involved with its global activities can yank on it, stop the line, and voice a suggestion without being ostracized? If not, perhaps you can move to get such a system implemented.

Other steps you might take to help your company globalize follow.

Create Synergy Between Corporate Parts

The legacy of Philips's corporate evolution provides a glimpse of what all globalizing firms—all 35,000 of them—are contending with: how to pursue more coordination among autonomous business units at the same time a firm widens its scope of business internationally. In short: How do you go global while remaining local—or, in Mohammed Ali's words, how do you get a monolithic corporation to "dance like a butterfly and sting like a bee"? In pursuit of this objective, CEOs are scything down vertical hierarchies to limit the number of decisions that must come down from on high, while preserving the benefits associated with being a multinational, like the ability to source and distribute inputs, technology, and capital globally. CEOs around the world are trying to retain characteristics of being small, nimble, and flexible, while their firms globalize and expand into new markets. Some U.S. firms are worthy of praise for cutting down their centralized administrative bureaucracies while gracefully globalizing, but many large firms find it hard to "deconstruct."

One method of integrating existing international operations into a global network is to set up a so-called matrix, or *mosaic*—a looser organizational structure in which the center knows what its parts are doing, yet allows its parts to do what they do autonomously. "We are not a global business," says Asea Brown Bovere CEO Perry Barnebik, whose firm is made up of 1,200 companies with its headquarters in Zurich. "We are a collection of local businesses with intense global coordination."[1] Responsibility for international activities is delegated to coordinated yet autonomous units; responsibility for service is driven down to the lowest possible rung in the hierarchy. AT&T has divided itself into 20 different product functions, each in command of its own marketing, pricing, R&D, and bottom line. Ford Motor Company, Digital, IBM, and Motorola are also "going mosaic" in the nineties.

Sometimes it's a case of the right hand not knowing what the left hand is doing. One of the authors (Engholm) introduced Science Applications International Corporation (SAIC) to a delegation of Chinese interested in purchasing the company's airport inspection system, which detects explosives in baggage. The Chinese team included high-level Chinese consulate officials who became keenly interested in SAIC's unique ownership and management structure. SAIC had an internal foundation that promoted the company's employee ownership (ESOP) model to other interested companies. As the company's representative in China, Engholm wanted to build SAIC's image in China by promoting its management model through its foundation.

The Chinese took the bait; the government was looking desperately for a way to reorganize the ownership of its state firms to increase efficiency, but in a way that did not appear to be outright capitalist privatization. SAIC's ESOP looked like a perfect model for the reform of China's state firms. The image-enhancement for SAIC in China would be enormous, and seminars to be run by SAIC's foundation to train the Chinese could be lucrative as well. Some weeks passed as the Chinese analyzed materials sent. Then suddenly, Engholm found out from the Chinese that they had contacted SAIC's foundation directly, and had even invited SAIC representatives to China to make a formal presentation. A foundation manager had actually *trained* a group of Chinese officials in how to set up an ESOP and had provided a copy of all relevant printed materials. SAIC had squandered a golden opportunity to promote itself in a country in which it was trying to sell $10 to $15 million worth of high-tech airport equipment. The Chinese went direct, and free-of-charge they obtained a week of training and all needed printed software. SAIC could be forgotten—and indeed it was.

Synergy means a lot more than just getting divisions to talk to one another. Executives should actively look for ways in which their divisions might augment each other, and thereby enlarge the pie. The business of international media entertainment is a prime example of how important it is to control a property as it moves through many media permutations. Sony tries to leverage its films and music divisions to enhance the yield of any given project, as well as tying in its manufacturing electronics. MCA and Matsushita have both become investors in the 3DO Company, which develops an interactive game system and software.

But the German media giant Bertelsmann, with $11 billion in sales, has shunned the notion of synergy. At least one of its executives has labeled the concept "a contradiction to focus." Starting in the early nineteenth century as a Christian book bindery business, the multinational is now involved in all aspects of media production, with pretax profits of over $635 million in 1993, $500 million in the bank, and zero debt. The management paradigm that is drilled into all 45,000 employees of the firm has prevented the firm from obtaining profitable synergy among its divisions. That corporate philosophy is based on the idea of *Betriebsergebnis*, which roughly translates as "return on assets." Each division manager understands that he must meet his *Betrieb*, a predeterminded rate of return that has been assigned for his operation, which, when all divisions obtain it, allows the parent to pay 15 percent returns to the holder of its profit-sharing certificates.

Each division is judged in terms of its bottom line such that little synergy between divisions occurs. Division leaders remain tightly focused on their own activities, and big opportunities have been missed because of this. As one top executive puts it: "[The company] undervalues a lot of media properties because they look at everything in isolation. They calculate current performance and then run the numbers out a few years, never taking into account any operating synergy or business combination." Business combinations were sorely missed when the company's Bantam Doubleday Dell book division racked up record sales of $650 million in 1993 with the bestsellers from John Grisham. The $3 billion (revenues) U.S.-based entertainment division of the company, called Bertelsmann Music Group, was unable to capitalize on this bookselling success. The rights were sold to Paramount to produce *The Firm*, which grossed $223 million at the box office in 1993. Meanwhile, the company's most successful record division, Arista, which is headed by legendary record mogul Clive Davis, has slipped out from under Bertelsmann's Prussian-style management doctrine to achieve $300 million in annual sales, while another music division, RCA Records, which has remained under the parent's thumb, has had three presidents in the last eight years and has seen its market share plummet.[2]

Bring Affiliates into the "Corporate Family"

If your firm wants to go global, rather than forcing its affiliates to abandon their mode of localism, or go to the other extreme of granting it complete autonomy, you must, as it were, bring them into the corporate family. You can help affiliates to perceive themselves as part of a global corporation to which they belong and have allegiances, rather than purely a local company, or one with its *own* global agenda.

Through a simple initiative to better communicate, you can impart a philosophy that says to every sibling company: The better each branch of the company does, the better every branch does. Imitate the approach of many Japanese companies; even those that do delegate authority tend to instill a big-picture feeling of unity among their parts.

Hold a companywide conference to generate unity of purpose and a sense of camaraderie among distant players. You can't just fax a manager in Kuwait that an affiliate of the company has an interesting product of which he should be aware. This manager must be brought into a conference setting and presented the corporate philosophy, becoming involved in the exchange process. Bring him into the family. Expose him to and train him in the product lines and services of the parent's other affiliates around the world. Introduce him to the managers of other plants in person. In this way, you create a forum for exchange between global units, which becomes part of the firm's corporate culture. For years, IBM has held regional sales conferences attended by hundreds of employees who participate in training and share their knowledge. Companies that have been involved in sales of consumer goods rather than capital goods are often more people-oriented than other companies and have done much more sales, cultural, and management training. But with the global spread of accounting, legal, and consulting activities, it's time for service companies to do the same.

You might consider putting in place a person with the title of International Operations Coordinator (or Global Resources Coordinator), responsible for generating communication, knowledge exchange, and coordinating activities between all parts of a global firm. Ideally, this person would be involved in global strategizing at the board level and not just a manager.

Set Up a System for Information Exchange

You can't cut costs and generate efficiency and economies of scale in the global sphere without effective communication among units. Gathering and exploiting global information is a critical challenge, part of the new game of acquiring knowledge capital through business alliances. "The game is shifting," says Christopher A. Bartlett, a specialist in international management at Harvard Business School, "from capturing benefits of scale to developing and diffusing the benefits of information. It was simple when it was all in the home market, but it is much tougher to use the world as a source of intelligence and expertise."[3] For the old-style manager, information is power and thus to be hoarded and protected. The objective for global firms is to turn this outmoded attitude around and get managers sharing information, especially across borders.

Open up communication channels and *democratize* them. Scores of firms have set up links through which two-way information and knowledge exchange among employees, affiliates, and customers can happen, and you can be instrumental in helping your company do likewise. Matsushita asked suppliers for input on improvements. GE Medical Systems conducts 1,000 hours of teleconferencing per year. One of Mexico's best-run companies, Cementos Mexicanos (CEMEX), monitors every facet of its global production network—down to the real-time monitoring, for example, of the energy consumption of any of its offshore factories—through an information system that sidesteps the hassles of communicating through the country's inefficient local phone system.[4]

Building communication links begins with a companywide E-mail system. E-mail is *the* cheap and fast method to link everyone in the corporation, though just getting everyone trained on programs like E-Mail or Lotus Notes can be a gargantuan undertaking for a firm with thousands of employees worldwide. On-line tutorials are in the works; Hewlett-Packard operates one that is broadcast from studios in the United States and Europe to trainees around the globe. A companywide satellite training network is next for some firms.

Video conferencing can be a method of erasing borders too. Johnson Electric of Hong Kong, the second largest producer of micromotors, has become so dispersed that its managing director, Patrick Wang, has set up a video conferencing system to link the company's R&D labs in Europe, factories in South China, engineers in Hong Kong, and customers in America and elsewhere.[5] Quality control and operations management get a lot easier when all parties can hear and see each other, and the product being built—all in real time, mind you—rather than conducting cross talk via fax.

Emphasize Central Direction, Not Tight Control

Slowly, multinational firms are delegating more responsibility, taking a longer-leash approach to granting authority to local managers. In fact, a past Japanese head of Sony Europe was removed for stating that "Tokyo made all the decisions." Headquarters claimed he didn't understand the structure of the company.[6] Still, Japanese multinationals rarely bring foreign managers into their top management ranks. Sony is an exception; it includes an American and a European on the parent company's board, and they run Sony's U.S. and European operations, respectively. Executive deputy president Tamotsu Iba summarizes a philosophy rarely articulated in Japan: "Recruit the best possible local management. From our experience, that's the best direction."[7]

Owens-Corning Fiberglass Corporation manages its business

units at arm's length in some Asian countries because decision makers there expect local representatives to be senior people empowered to make decisions on their own. The company posts a "senior guy" locally in China because, as Owens-Corning's Asia Pacific president Charles R. Bland says, "If you have to check back with your boss, it compromises your credibility."[8]

Especially in emerging markets where the just-surfacing opportunities can be perceived only by those who are there on the ground, reward your autonomous units for being nimble opportunists, encouraging them to seek out deals within, as well as outside, their specified functional areas. Let them put together the human, financial, and technical resources to make an innovative deal work. Charoen Pokphand, the multitentacled Thai conglomerate said to be the leading investor in China, allows company "groups" to act something like investment companies, spotting opportunities and then cobbling together the "people, money, and technology needed to exploit them."[9]

But delicate is the art of letting local deal making go wild and then reeling it in later. Matsushita's $6.1 billion acquisition of MCA was fraught with clashes between the parent's staid and risk-averse Japanese decision-making style and the faster-paced top-down style of MCA's top executives, Sidney J. Sheinberg and Lew R. Wasserman. The merger was a disaster for Matsushita, and all of the deal's supporters have been purged from the parent's board of directors. The relationship came to the breaking point when the MCA boys wanted to buy a 25 percent share in a U.S. television network in late 1994; Matsushita executives had already squashed two previous proposals presented by MCA, a $600 million proposal to buy Virgin Records and a $50 million one to buy a 20 percent share of a theme park venture in Japan. When Sheinberg and his negotiators visited Matsushita to talk about the idea, President Yoichi Morishita sent in a team of lackeys to inform the Americans their proposal had been turned down. The no-nonsense Sheinberg was livid. Then Morishita entered the room and said: "I see you've been told." For its part, MCA felt treated like a poor relation. "It was not what they did, but the style," says Sheinberg. Matsushita blames Japan's bubble economy for not wanting to spend big on MCA's deal making.[10] In spring of 1995, Matsushita decided to cut its losses and sold its controlling interest to Seagram. In spite of great sums of money (it was the most expensive purchase a Japanese company has made in the United States), extreme optimism, and genuine good intentions, the venture failed without either understanding the culture of the other.

Organized corporate team-building sessions designed to bring disparate corporate cultures together are the remedy for some corporations now owned by, or joint venturing with, a foreign company. Some Japanese companies in the United States, such as NEC, Mitsubishi, Panasonic, and TDK, bring their cross-cultural management teams into a closer relationship by bringing in outside trainers to teach each about others' business cultures and to work together creatively to solve problems. The gamut of team-building exercises runs from this sort of high-level seminar to the "ropes-course retreat," where members of the same global conglomerate learn about risk and team effort close to nature. In a typical exercise, teams work to connect planks to cross a river. In an exercise concocted for a large telecommunications company, teams work together with a box of PVC pipe to successfully transport a tennis ball across a hotel swimming pool "completely dry." If President Clinton can consort with late-night infomercial self-help motivational guru Anthony Robbins at Camp David, corporations should feel perfectly comfortable and beyond reproach for trying out any technique that might generate synergy between their international affiliates, no matter how peculiar or unorthodox.

Skunk Groups and Mentoring

Skunk groups are teams of people given a loosely specified objective and the resources to achieve it outside the company hierarchy. Nascent global management models try to emphasize team dynamics. Managers dispatch "swat teams" of internationally savvy staff or hired guns to open new markets. Unilever sends in an "A-team" to open China; Texas Instruments sends a team of its so-called nomads overseas; other companies hire a consultant with in-country experience to get an operation going, as IBM has by sending experienced consultant William Howell to Hanoi. These teams should be global in vision, experienced in emerging markets, and well trained in the country in question. One member of the team should be a person in your salesforce—a quick thinker. Group tasks should be rotated so that each group begins to take on a more general knowledge of the workings of the overseas venture.

After the swat team goes in, you need to recruit and mentor. Motorola promotes worker loyalty in Malaysia by rewarding good ideas with hard cash, actively listening to employee suggestions (there have been 41,000 of them), and dividing its Penang workforce into teams with names like The Roadrunners and The Orient Express. Applicants are appraised, in part, on their willingness to be part of a team. Workers and managers are also brought back to headquarters for training and 18-month mentorships.[11]

The Japanese are especially serious about mentoring. An incredible amount of it goes on in the typical large Japanese organization. When a worker takes a position in a Japanese company, for example, he or she may spend an entire year in orientation. A fledgling representative is often sent to a foreign country for a year or more to simply live in the culture before taking on a business function there. Just "making connections" is part of the Japanese overseas business approach; a hiree's mandate actually might be to "go to Brazil and make connections."

Set up a system that rewards mentoring. Employees must feel they have something to gain by becoming a mentor for another person. This motivation tends not to exist in U.S. companies because such mentoring would be on the person's own time. But mentorships are built into Japanese corporate organization, and the mentoring is part of the mentors' salaried time.

Also, you should never remove an international representative from his or her local relationships abruptly and then send in a new person to start from scratch. You have to have the new person introduced and apprised of who the local people are, why each person is important, who they are connected to—all of which can take years for a representative to figure out in another culture.

Recruiting and Training Your International Staff

Akio Morita, the illustrious late president of Sony, when asked why he demanded to personally interview all new recruits, quipped: "The future prosperity of Sony rests in the hands of the last person we recruited."

Indeed, special care must be taken in the hiring of people who will be asked to interact with people from other countries and other cultures. Mepco's Frank Burham would agree that one bad apple can spoil the bunch! He would also agree that it's wise to fill many headquarter positions with people who have worked overseas, so cultural sensitivity gets passed down.

Although your people will certainly vary in the amount of interaction they will have with foreign clients—from the person who visits a customer in a single country once in a while, to the vice president of an international division who travels overseas repeatedly during the year, to the expatriate who actually relocates to the country on a permanent basis—every person on your staff should be hired with some degree of cultural adaptability in mind.

Selecting people for overseas postings has become a sophisticated process because of the high costs associated with failure. Firms test the recruit, and his or her family as well, for characteristics associated with overseas success. Mike Lorelli acknowledges that "for putting somebody in a headquarters job where they will be interacting with a ton of countries, it's not as risky." But, if you're going to send an American with his family to work in Taiwan ten years, that's a whole different ball game. Says Lorelli: "Then, we'll put them through a test—to help them as much as to help us. Do they really have that adaptability? Presuming that they test well, then we'll put them through a two- or three-week training for the person and his or her whole family."

In choosing expatriates and country representatives, too many companies depend on the language criteria. Language fluency is hardly a requisite for success, although it does help immensely in forging informal relationships. Skill and experience in the specific industry and market in the country in question are paramount. Don't send a middle manager with a background as an accountant or lawyer to manage a plant, just because he or she speaks the local language. In most cases send the practioner, not the theorist—the person who has worked the whole assembly line from top to bottom, who gets under the machines, gets grease under his nails. A solid, hands-on knowledge of the production line earns the foreign manager the acceptance and respect he or she will need to make changes in an enterprise.

One key consideration must be acknowledged before hiring someone to work overseas: Does he or she possess an extraordinarily patient and tolerant disposition? Some people have infinite patience; nothing surprises them. Others lose composure easily, and in worst-case scenarios, bad-mouth the locals. Nothing can do the image of your firm more harm. A U.S. commercial officer in Seoul said:

> You have to be unflappable. Many foreign businesspeople here get mad. They want trade sanctions imposed. They're

tough, impatient, sue-'em types. They go Section 301 when disputes arise, and sometimes they win. They phone the president of the United States and the secretary of state to get things done. Sometimes it works. But if you can't call the president, you're better off being patient and working within the system.

In an initial private interview, inquire about the candidate's personal circumstances, including family situation, financial status, children's schooling, and medical history. Any major dilemma in these areas will deprive the person of time to do the job. The reason for failure most often cited in our interviews was dissatisfaction on the part of the spouse. If the spouse can't assimilate or doesn't want to raise the children away from home or is for any other reason dissatisfied, the pressure on the executive can be too much to bear. Ask the candidate why he or she wants to work overseas and compare expectations about the position against what you know to be the reality of working in the country. Is the person tolerant of others and of different ways of doing things? Does the person possess a positive outlook on life in general?

Don't hire people because they are good *here.* They may not be good *there.* Use criteria based on the requirements of the host culture. This information is readily available from professional trainers, other staff who have worked overseas, books, and the country's natives who work at your company. A variety of assessment instruments are used by companies as predictive tools, but it requires a deep and comprehensive study of a person's characteristics to achieve predictive validity. Don't depend on simplistic in-house assessment tools.

Once you've hired your international staff, you must consider such types of training as cross-cultural training, language training, country-specific business briefings, seminars on foreign business culture and practices, repatriation preparation, and cultural diversity awareness-building programs. Country-specific trainings provide staff with deep background about a country, its business culture, how to communicate and negotiate with the people, and a briefing about essential business protocol. Diversity training helps people appreciate the challenges faced by immigrants, diffuse stereotypical thinking, clarify their own values and resulting behaviors, facilitate communication between native and non-native English speakers, and accurately interpret the behaviors and expectations of workers from diverse cultures. Foreign-assignment training provides future expatriates with knowledge of the logistics of living in the host country, the challenges a family will face and the best methods for dealing with them, and the personal aspects of making the relocation smooth and productive. Destination assistance for relocating employees helps with finding housing, schools for children, the physical move, and the like.

To make cost-effective decisions about training, human resources managers might consider administering a cross-cultural corporate assessment instrument. This is a way to find out where a firm stands in terms of multicultural expertise. Administered individually or in groups, it can gauge skills, define areas of activity, and indicate, in visual form, where the need for training exists. It allows companies to implement training programs in an orchestrated manner, increase efficiency, and cut costs.

What is the average cost of training? A typical day fee for a cross-cultural or country-specific training from a reputable company will cost your firm between $3,000 and $4,500, plus materials and travel expenses for the trainer(s). One company paid $16,000 to a prominent training company for a two-day training on Malaysian business culture, including four *facilitators,* who ran the training, and one *resource person* originally from Malaysia with in-country expertise.

To further facilitate the international education of your staff, consider these ideas:

• Start an international library and subscribe to a database for use by your international staff.

- Purchase videotapes that portray international bargaining styles, protocol, and travel tips.
- Sponsor in-house language courses.
- Start an E-mail bulletin board for sharing international information.
- Invite lunchtime speakers, possibly members of your own staff or that of another division, to share their overseas experiences.
- Require staff to attend World Trade Organization conferences.
- If your budget can handle it, send key people to corporate seminars sponsored by a major university. The IBEAR program held each summer at the University of Southern California is one example.

Make the Foreign Posting a Promotion

In 1989, James E. Challenger, president of the outplacement firm Gray & Christmas in Chicago, said of working overseas, "I advise everyone against it. It's one of the most dead-end things you can do."[12] Amazingly, given the global era we have entered, American workers and managers continue to feel that to accept an international assignment means they will be passed up in the next round of promotions. Again and again, we hear that if you want to further your career, don't take an international assignment; "If you're out of sight, you're out of mind." Although CEOs pay lip service to the notion that top managers should possess international experience, many have returned from overseas postings to find that their underlings have filled top slots.

Is working a stint overseas a good way to get forgotten? We talked to Karen Rakita at Hughes Space and Communications Company and she agreed that it was. "Your day-to-day activities, be they good or bad, are not seen and any information on your performance will be second- or thirdhand. And when you are done with your assignment, you don't always know where you're going to work. It's not that when people come back they are out of a job; it's just that there is some scrambling to try and figure out where we're going to put this person because all of a sudden they're back and we need to re-integrate them."

Not everyone agrees. "I think [taking an international position] is an absolute must," says Mike Lorelli. "An absolute must."

"At Chevron," says John Haglund, "the international path has always been a good one." The problem is that it's historically difficult to do so because Chevron's overseas units tend to develop their own people and have not brought in people from the outside. According to Haglund, another issue has been downsizing, which has removed many internationally oriented people from their jobs at Chevron.

Multinationals are learning hard lessons nowadays. To forget about their overseas staff is tantamount to losing them to hungry placement companies even before they return home. Hanoi and Saigon have recently become the poaching capitals of the world where twenty-somethings with one year of in-country experience change jobs constantly in search of the best salary, benefits, and profit-sharing. Some firms have responded. As early as 1990, Dow Chemical, 3M, and Bechtel put in place policies for keeping people in the promotional pipeline while they perform stints abroad.

At your firm, is the foreign posting viewed as a promotion or a form of career purgatory? You might encourage those in charge at your company to consider the following suggestions:

1. Make being sent overseas a carrot and not a stick. Don't send people whom you want to get rid of; send your best. They will be in demand when they return rather than feel they are forgotten deadwood. You want people competing to go, not competing to stay.

2. Extend the amount of time the employee will remain in the country beyond the normal three to five years. Nothing threatens

the delicate relationship between the parent company and its foreign counterpart more than expatriate turnover. But keep them in the circuit by bringing them to headquarters regularly.

3. Set up an international personnel services branch to handle relocation, banking, home management, vacations, and so on. Some companies guarantee expatriates an equal or higher paying job when they return. Others assist with the problems of reentry, transferring and translating medical records in a foreign language, taking the kids out of school and getting them into a new one, moving furniture home, leaving close friends and making new ones.

Is the International for You?

Working overseas stirs the adventurousness in all of us. There is perhaps no faster way to deepen one's skill base and business expertise than to spend a year or two working in another country and learning a foreign language. And the growth of the international jobs market seems set to continue into the next century. NYNEX has 103 U.S. executives overseas, whereas it had very few in the early 1990s. Dell Computer employs "dozens of Americans abroad," while in the late 1980s it had only a handful. The trend will continue because experienced local managers just don't exist in countries like Poland, Ukraine, and Vietnam. Companies continue to find that they must send in Americans to spearhead the local effort.

But there are drawbacks to this position. The first is that while the total number of expatriates has expanded with globalization, the new ones cannot expect the perks that earlier generations enjoyed. They once had leverage to bargain for contract clauses guaranteeing incentive compensation, housing allowance, hardship allowance, position allowance, taxation allowance, relocation expenses, foreign language instruction, cross-cultural training, vacation and home leave, and children's education expense. For most, those days have vanished. The fat expat package is disappearing as companies find competent locals to hire. Take Proctor & Gamble in Geneva. In the 1960s, most bosses were American and few were fluent in French. They lived in American-style suburban homes like pampered princes. Now, most P&G executives in Europe are Europeans, who are both cheaper and more familiar with the local culture.

Michael A. Pappan is vice chairman-international at Ward Howell, an executive search organization. Although more than half of the firm's international search assignments are looking for local nationals, "there are certain positions that the local national can't fill," says Pappan. "Like being the general manager of an operation in Hungary [because] it's very unlikely that we're going to find somebody in Hungary, unless he has spent a lot of time in the West." In fact, a joint venture should have both local staff people who understand the locals, and people from the home office who can change the culture of the company.

Here's what search organizations are looking for. First, language ability and cultural knowledge based on years lived abroad as well as experience as a manager. "What we're looking for," says Pappan, "once you get beyond the technological training and some language and cultural affinity, is management ability—success as a manager in a Western organization—someone who has proved that he can run something, an effective motivator who is organized and can build a business." The new expatriates are required to be independent doers, self-motivated, noncorporate, superresourceful, trustworthy, adept at crossing culture and bilingual barriers, with the patience of Job, able to forge and maintain connections, and willing to rough it. The new expatriate is indeed a hybrid, many of them foreign-born Americans—like Vietnamese-Americans, Chinese-Americans, and Latinos—who will have an edge because of their fluency in others' languages and their familiarity with other cultures. "I think like a Westerner," says Imrich Gombar, director of human relations for K-Mart in Czechoslovakia, "but I work like a local."[13]

Part I: Assessing Your Commitment to International Excellence

Answer each item by circling the appropriate number on the continuum below:

To Almost No Extent		To Some Extent		To a Great Extent		To a Very Great Extent	
1 2	3	4 5	6	7	8	9	10

I seek out people in my company who can inform me about what the firm is doing overseas and to help me build my international expertise.

1   2   3   4   5   6   7   8   9   10

I make efforts to help my colleagues prepare for interacting with overseas businesspeople to prevent miscommunication and blunders.

1   2   3   4   5   6   7   8   9   10

I have a personal plan for enhancing my global skills now and in the future.

1   2   3   4   5   6   7   8   9   10

I have thought about what my company needs to do to achieve more globally and have made my ideas known to decision makers.

1   2   3   4   5   6   7   8   9   10

When I consider voting for a political candidate, I look at his or her position on U.S. industrial policy, international trade, and global outlook.

1   2   3   4   5   6   7   8   9   10

Part II: Assessing Your Company for Commitment to International Excellence

My firm has a clear idea about the challenges it faces in making changes in its overall management structure in order to best respond to globalization.

1   2   3   4   5   6   7   8   9   10

The upper management of my firm has made a concerted attempt to instill commitment to globalization among each and every one of its employees.

1   2   3   4   5   6   7   8   9   10

My firm has put in place an electronic bulletin board (or other system) whereby international staff can post notes about their experience in a country, share useful tips and insights, and exchange information about company activities there.

1   2   3   4   5   6   7   8   9   10

My firm offers its expatriate families extensive orientation training before sending them overseas to live, and acknowledges the risk and high cost of its representatives being afflicted by "culture shock."

1   2   3   4   5   6   7   8   9   10

My firm is active in informing U.S. government agencies about its position on issues affecting its international business.

1   2   3   4   5   6   7   8   9   10

Now add up your score. If you assessed yourself or your firm at 25 or lower out of a possible total of 50, the area of commitment to international excellence should be a key priority at your company.

Committing Your Country
to Globalism

No one nation, one company, or one person can stand alone against the world for very long. In the global era, countries will protect their sovereignty by becoming members of groups of nations. Pure economic nationalism belongs to history. All countries are dependent on others to an ever-increasing degree and are thus vulnerable to political instability in them, environmental damage caused by them, and economic problems faced by them.

Governments, like businesses and like people, have had to adopt a mentality of alliance. Global politics, like global business, must now be approached as a win/win proposition in forums of consensus building. Our government must change its mentality, change its vocabulary for engaging with others. We can no longer afford to be parochial in outlook and equivocal in the messages we send overseas. Teaming up, synergy, mutual cooperation and benefit, partnership, and relationship are the watchwords of this new era.

A sign of our interdependence: the fall of the peso by one-third in early 1995 produced an instant loss of $10 billion for U.S. investors in Mexico, threatened NAFTA, and bankrupted scores of Mexican firms. Recognizing its economic symbiosis with the Mexican economy, the United States injected billions to boost the peso. GATT is another example of America's fading hegemony and emerging need to play as an equal among nations. GATT is a 22,500-page agreement that mandates $744 billion in tariff cuts and is estimated to add an annual $500 billion to the world's economy by 2005. It is the most comprehensive trade agreement in history, and it will earn this country $120 billion per year, the equivalent of 2 percent of our total GDP. As a member of GATT's regulatory agency, the World Trade Organization, the United States will have only one vote rather than a weighted vote commensurate with the size of its economy. One country, one vote. This will be the first time we participate in an international organization that formulates binding trade regulations. Says author Pat Choate: "For the first time in our history, a foreign body will have the right to hear challenges to any U.S. law and rule against it as an obstacle to trade. . . . [W]e will have no more power than any other country in the world."[1] (Readers should note, however, that any member of the WTO can back out of the organization by giving six months' notice; America's membership hardly represents the threat to U.S. sovereignty that GATT opponents have suggested.)

How the West deals as an interdependent player in this emerging world, especially the undeveloped world, will, to a great extent, be the measure of how well we do as business owners, managers, and workers. America, which has traditionally associated "national security" with maintaining sole control of its destiny (not to mention the destiny of its self-assigned hemisphere), has turned to alliances with other nations as a way to strengthen its position. Taking the lead in NAFTA, FATAA, and APEC are all moves for which the Clinton administration should be applauded. On the other hand, American foreign policy still rests on the country-centric notion that the United States "is the world's policeman" and definer of "the new world order" and, generally, the ideal to which all other nations should aspire. This attitude encourages jingoism and haughtiness in our international dealings with other nations, not to mention what Clyde Prestowitz in his book *Trading Places* has termed the "doctrinaire" attitude of our international representatives.

Our government still grapples with the problem of "the vision thing." We were totally without a vision for what the new world order was to look like after we won the Cold War. And we still don't have one. "Having won the cold war," wrote the novelist John Le Carré in a *New York Times* editorial, "the West can't afford to walk away from the consequences of its victory: whether we are speaking of Bosnia, Chechnya or Ingushetia or Cuba." We find it easier to play the ostrich than face global migraines like world famine, independence movements flaring everywhere, the world-wide poisoning of the earth and razing of its forests, and the growing volatility of the world's monetary system—all of which have as much impact on our national survival as arms proliferation.

Rather than become an enlightened steward of world human and natural resource development, the West has continued fighting the Cold War by nonmilitary means, mainly by isolating nations or arming them, trading with them or starving them of the cash they need to develop. The U.S. government effectively delayed the rebuilding of Vietnam for 20 years by prohibiting international lending organizations like the World Bank from lending money to the country to construct roads and provide health care. It crippled business efforts with a trade embargo that never achieved its initial objective. We have now given our policy of isolating Cuba to dislodge Castro about 35 years to take effect and it hasn't. American "legislators and policy makers," said a *New York Times* editorial recently, "seem to believe that the strategy that has worked for the rest of the Communist world—the opening of markets and the free exchange of goods, people and ideas—is somehow inappropriate for this one small island."[2] We are delaying the development of Cuba just like we did in Vietnam; meanwhile, Canada, Spain, and other countries get a jump on business deals in these emerging markets.

Our policy of isolating political enemies harms our competitiveness and is just downright inhumane. In 1994, one of the authors received a request for funding of a hospital in the city of Tianjin, China. Government officials in the city wanted to know if the U.S. government could provide the funding for the hospital with the stipulation that American construction firms and an American hospital would be contracted to build and administrate the hospital.

Engholm contacted USAID, the U.S. agency responsible for making loans of a humanitarian nature to foreign nations. "Sorry," came the reply. "We make no loans to China because we are prohibited from making loans to communist nations." The officials in Tianjin were aghast because they had recently received a similar loan from the Japanese government, which, incidentally, provided lucrative contracts to Japanese construction firms.

We are high-handed in our economic relations with the emerging world, focusing on the (albeit important) economic tasks of debt scheduling and stabilizing currencies, rather than providing the essential training and institutions necessary for real capitalism. We need to assist in institution building—the transfer of our culture of capitalism—rather than stuff inhumane "shock therapy" formulas down the throats of peoples and cultures.

You should encourage the U.S. government to do the following:

• Provide better support for American business in emerging markets such as Chile, Brazil, Vietnam, Poland, South Africa in the form of commercial attachés and stronger government-to-government relations.

• Provide more, and more timely, information to American businesspeople about emerging markets, rather than trim the amount provided, as has been done recently.

• Send high-level representatives to meet with the leaders of emerging countries to initiate commercial ties and high-profile joint projects, rather than send State Department types bent on discussing "security issues" and unprepared to discuss our economic relationship.

• Court investment from overseas by assisting local and state government officials to seek investment from foreign nations. South Carolina has been so successful in attracting German firms with its low wages (about 35 percent below German levels), tax breaks, and plans to improve its roads and schools, that one of its roads leading to a cluster of German factories is called the Autobahn.

• Provide more low-interest loans and loan guarantees to American companies, especially for sales into emerging countries. Concessionary financing is more readily available to our competitors.

Clearly, there will be no free lunch in the global economy. Competition will be fierce as so many more player nations and people enter the arena. The tough battles over the Canadian-U.S. Free Trade Agreement, NAFTA, and GATT have been good for the soul of America. We have chosen to lead rather than follow in the process of world integration. Our people have correctly recognized that more good new jobs can be created in America by becoming a member of free trade areas than by building higher fences around ourselves. Wages cannot be protected any more than markets can. If we want to sell our goods and service to others, our wages cannot be artificially pegged high.

Nor can we tolerate unfair mercantilist trade practices among our partners. Nor lax environmental protection policies. Nor gross violations of human rights. America has a $30 billion trade deficit with China, as of 1994, triple the 1990 level—while China's human rights record worsens. Moreover, our deficit with Japan was $66 billion in 1994 and is unlikely to decline in 1995.

The new order cannot afford to allow there to be winner and loser nations. The potential for cataclysmic instability and conflict is too high. Win/win is our only hope. Profit making *can* be accomplished in a responsible manner, with global consciousness guiding us. The disenfranchised can be looked after, cared for, and assisted in joining the family of nations, firms, and organizations, which, together, can steer spaceship earth. And internationally aware businesses can be the key mode by which this vision is realized.

The process begins with people like you.

NOTES

Introduction

[1] Mark Pendergrast, *For God, Country, and Coca-Cola: The Unauthorized History of the Great American Soft Drink and the Company That Makes It* (New York: Charles Scribner's Sons, 1993), p. 377.

Strategy I

[1] Richard J. Barnet and John Cavanagh, *Global Dreams: Imperial Corporations and the New World Order* (New York: Simon and Schuster, 1994), p. 104.

[2] Alvin Toffler, *PowerShift: Knowledge, Wealth, and Violence at the Edge of the 21st Century* (New York: Bantam, 1990), pp. 226–27.

[3] Ibid.

[4] Louis Kraar, "The Overseas Chinese," *Fortune*, 31 October 1994, p. 98.

[5] Shuji Hayashi, *Culture and Management in Japan* (New York: Columbia University Press, 1986).

[6] William Echikson, "Young Americans Go Abroad to Strike It Rich," *Fortune*, 17 October 1994, p. 186.

[7] Toffler, p. 28.

[8] "High-Tech Jobs All Over the Map," *Business Week*, 21st Century Capitalism issue, 1994, p. 119.

[9] Echikson, p. 187.

[10] Amanda Bennett, "An Economist Investigates the Irrationality of People," *Wall Street Journal*, 29 July 1994, p. B1.

[11] Kraar, p. 102.

[12] Brenton R. Schlender, "How Toshiba Makes Alliances Work," *Fortune*, 4 October 1993, pp. 116–20.

[13] "Tearing Up Today's Organization Chart," *Business Week*, 21st Century Capitalism issue, 1994, p. 86.

[14] John Naisbitt, *Global Paradox: The Bigger the World Economy, the More Powerful Its Smallest Players* (New York: William Morrow, 1994), p. 20.

Strategy II

[1] This quote comes from an unpublished paper by John L. Graham called "Vis-à-Vis," p. 27.

[2] This excerpt was reprinted in Harper's "Readings," October 1994, p. 14.

Strategy V

[1] *New York Times Magazine,* 6 June 1990, p. 49.

[2] George C. Greanian, *The Foreign Corrupt Practices Act* (New York: D. C. Heath and Co., 1982), p. 75.

[3] Robert Lacey, *The Kingdom: Arabia and the House of Sa'ud* (New York: Harcourt Brace Jovanovich, 1981), pp. 469–70.

[4] Philip R. Cateora, *International Marketing* (Homewood, Ill.: Irwin, 1990), p. 131.

[5] This definition is taken from an internal code of conduct manual distributed by Chevron Oil Company to its employees.

[6] Richard J. Barnet and John Cavanagh, *Global Dreams: Imperial Corporations and the New World Order* (New York: Simon and Schuster, 1994), p. 18.

[7] Alvin Toffler, *PowerShift: Knowledge, Wealth, and Violence at the Edge of the 21st Century* (New York: Bantam, 1990), p. 27.

[8] Paul Kennedy, *Preparing for the 21st Century* (New York: Random House, 1994), p. 56.

[9] Michael Parrish and William R. Long, "Villagers Stand Up to Big Oil," *Los Angeles Times,* 6 November 1994, p. A18.

[10] *New York Times,* 1 August 1994, p. C1.

[11] Anthony Sampson, *Black and Gold: Tycoons, Revolutionaries, and Apartheid* (New York: Pantheon, 1987), pp. 24–28.

Strategy VII

[1] John Naisbitt, *Global Paradox: The Bigger the World Economy, the More Powerful Its Smallest Players* (New York: William Morrow, 1994), p. 19.

[2] Matthew Schifrin, "The Betriebsergebnis Factor," *Forbes,* 24 May 1994, pp. 118–24.

[3] "Tearing Up Today's Organization Chart," *Business Week,* 21st Century Capitalism issue, 1994, p. 83.

[4] Ibid., p. 86.

[5] Louis Kraar, "The Overseas Chinese," *Fortune,* 31 October 1994, p. 98.

[6] Richard J. Barnet and John Cavanagh, *Global Dreams: Imperial Corporations and the New World Order* (New York: Simon and Schuster, 1994), p. 16.

[7] "Tearing Up Today's Organization Chart," p. 90.

[8] Ibid., p. 83.

[9] "Competing for Asia," *The Economist*, 26 November 1994, p. 16.

[10] Geraldine Fabrikant and Andrew Pollack, "MCA's Impatience with Wary Parent," *New York Times*, 4 November 1994, p. C1.

[11] "Importing Enthusiasm," *Business Week*, 21st Century Capitalism issue, 1994, p. 122.

[12] *Investor's Daily*, 18 September 1989, p. 1.

[13] William Echikson, "Young Americans Go Abroad to Strike It Rich," *Fortune*, 17 October 1994, p. 194.

Afterword

[1] James Risen, "New Trade Body's Power Called Overrated," *Los Angeles Times*, 2 December 1994, p. A18.

[2] "The U.S. and Cuba: Double Fantasy," *New York Times*, 14 December 1994, p. A18.

INDEX

CEMEX (Cementos Mexicanos), 197
Census Bureau, 14
centralized management, 32–33, 198–99
Challenger, James E., 206
Charoen Pokphand Group, 35
Chase Manhattan Bank, 153
Chevron, 32–33, 65–66, 131–32, 134, 207
Chile, 215
China, 5, 8–9, 20, 24–26, 33, 35, 58, 63, 65, 90, 175, 199
    business cards in, 161
    and diaspora populations, 44
    and ethical issues, 125–27, 139, 143–46, 152, 216
    and import-export entrepreneurs, 29–30
    and international loans, 214–15
    and language/communications issues, 96, 97
    MFN status of, 152
    and protocol issues, 161, 169, 172, 173, 178
    and SAIC, 193–94
    trade deficit with, 216
    Unilever in, 201
Choate, Pat, 213
Chronowski, Barbara, 37
Citibank, 23
class divisions, 58, 148–50
classified information, 112–13
cleanliness, 163–64
Clinton, Bill, 9, 131, 152, 200, 213
clothing, appropriate, 165–66
Coca-Cola, 5–6, 36, 90
Cohen, Gary, 138

Cold War, 5, 17, 18, 213–14
communication. See also etiquette; language
    asking questions, 86, 90, 108–9, 113, 117
    and confrontation vs. consensus, 80–81
    and foreign employees, 92–93
    and humor, 82–83
    and implicit vs. explicit styles, 75–77
    and linear vs. polychronic styles, 78–79
    nonverbal, 93–99, 171–72
    and the public vs. the private self, 79–80
    and setting up systems for information exchange, 197–98
    skills, overview of, 83–88
    and style and pacing, 81–82, 84–85
    things that subvert, 90–91
    and using interpreters, 88–90
Comparator Systems Corporation, 146
confidentiality, 112–13
Confucianism, 18, 156
contradiction, tolerance for, 56
Copal, 185–89
Corning, 48–49, 50–51, 54
Cuba, 19, 214
cultural relations, 10, 48–69
    and cross-cultural training, 64–69
    and deep culture, 62
    and ethnocentrism, 44, 51–54
    and humor, 82–83
    and stereotyping, 54–57

Tungsram, 34
Turkey, 101

Ueshiba, Morihei, 117
Ukraine, 208
Uniden, 35
Unilever, 201
Union Carbine, 143
United Kingdom, 145, 168–69. *See also* Britain; England
United Nations, 6, 146–47
universal perspective, 18–20
University of California at Irvine, 95
University of Southern California, 206
USAID, 215
U.S. Overseas Private Investment Corporation, 22–23
Uzbekistan, 72–73

Varshney, Ashutosh, 152
Vietnam, 60, 63–64, 92, 129–32, 141, 145, 148, 208, 214–15
Virgin Records, 199
Vitro, 48–49, 50–51, 54

vocabulary, simplifying, 85
Volkswagen, 35

Wal-Mart, 34–35
Wang, Patrick, 198
Waotrani natives, 66–68, 148
Warsaw Stock Exchange, 7
Wasserman, Lew R., 199
Watergate Scandal, 135
weaknesses, minimizing, 26–30
Weatherford, Jack, 42, 44
Wedel factory, 7
Wherry, Kenneth, 16–17
women, advice for, 99–101, 165
World Bank, 146, 214
World Economic System, 18
worldviews, 15–30
World War I, 17
World War II, 17, 65
WTO, 18, 206, 213
Wu, Golden, 35

Xerox, 3, 149

yin-yang concept, 56–57
Young, Andrew, 128

About the Authors

DIANA ROWLAND is a cross-cultural trainer relying on more than 25 years of international experience and is author of the best-selling book *Japanese Business Etiquette: A Practical Guide to Success with the Japanese* (Warner Books, 1993). She has been featured in *Fortune, Esquire, Japan Newsweek, The International Herald Tribune, The Asian Wall Street Journal,* and on *The MacNeil/Lehrer Newshour.*

Ms. Rowland is president of Rowland & Associates, which provides a wide variety of cross-cultural training. Clients include: Chevron, Georgia Power, Hughes, ITT, Levi Strauss, Northern Telecom, and Panasonic. She is also on the faculty of Pacific Rim Management Programs at the University of Southern California.

CHRISTOPHER ENGHOLM is founder of The Engholm Group in Del Mar, Calfornia, which specializes in market reserch and company representation in Asia and Latin America. He has conducted international business consulting and seminars for firms such as Hughes, Chevron, and Science Applications International Corporation, and is a frequent speaker on the topics of emerging markets, business culture, and protocol.

He has written seven other books, including *When Business East Meets Business West: The Guide to Practice and Protocol in the Pacific Rim, The Asia and Japan Business Information Sourcebook,* and *Doing Business in Asia's Booming "China Triangle."*

TAKING STOCK

A good first step in moving your corporation toward international excellence is to take inventory of the current situation in your company, assessing gaps between the expertise people currently have and the expertise they need in order to best conduct their work activities with people of other cultures.

For a snapshot of your corporation's readiness to conduct its cross-cultural work effectively, pick a group of 100–2,000 people that you work with. On a separate sheet of paper, respond to the following items regarding this group and mail to Rowland & Associates, Inc., 6920 Miramar Road, Suite 308, San Diego, CA 92121. Please include your name, title, and telephone number, and make sure your current address appears on the letterhead.

1. The group I am answering these questions for is my _____ (department, division, company, etc.).

2. There are _____ (*indicate number*) people in this group.

3. _____ % of these people interact with people who live in other countries.

4. _____ % of these people work in a domestic multicultural workforce.

5. _____ % of these people are familiar with the concepts and skills discussed in this book.

6. _____ (*indicate number*) people in this group work with several cultures of one specific region of the world.

7. _____ % of these people appear to be extremely effective at working with people from that area.

8. _____ (*indicates number*) people in our group work with only one foreign culture.

9. _____ % of these people appear to be extremely effective at working with people from that culture.

10. We plan to relocate _____ (*indicate number of employees and family members*) people abroad in the next two years.

11. _____ % of our group is intensively involved in negotiation, technology transfer, and/or giving presentations to people who live in other countries.

12. We have _____ (*indicate number*) people involved in cross-cultural or multinational teams.